D0387496

A–Z

of Film, Television and Video Terms

Also available from Blueprint

Pocket Glossary of Advertising Terms
Pocket Glossary of Computer Terms for
                    Printers and Publishers
Pocket Glossary of Printing, Binding and Paper Terms
Pocket Glossary of Publishing Terms
Pocket Glossary of Design and Typographic Terms

A–Z

of Film, Television and Video Terms

Alex Bushby

BLUEPRINT
An Imprint of Chapman & Hall

London • Glasgow • New York • Tokyo • Melbourne • Madras

**Published by Blueprint, and imprint of Chapman & Hall,
2 – 6 Boundary Row, London SE1 8HN**

Chapman & Hall, 2 – 6 Boundary Row, London SE1 8HN, UK

Blackie Academic & Professional, Wester Cleddens Road,
Bishopbriggs, Glasgow G64 2NZ, UK

Chapman & Hall Inc., One Penn Plaza, 41st Floor,
New York NY10119, USA

Chapman & Hall Japan, Thomson Publishing Japan, Hirakawacho
Nemoto Building, 6F, 1-7-11 Hirakawa-cho, Chiiyoda-ku,
Tokyo 1022, Japan

Chapman & Hall Australia, Thomas Nelson Australia,
102 Dodds Street, South Melbourne, Victoria 3205, Australia

Chapman & Hall India, R. Seshadri, 32 Second Main Road, CIT East,
Madras 600 035, India

First edition 1994
© 1994 Alex Bushby

ISBN 0 948905 8 91
Printed in Great Britain by St Edmunsbury Press,
Bury St. Edmunds, Suffolk

A catalogue record for this book is available from the British Library.
Library of Congress Catalog Card Number available.

Printed on Acid-free text paper, manufactured in accordance with
ANSI/NISO Z39.48-1992 (Permanence of Paper).

[Paper = Fineblade, 100 gsm]

A

A
AUDIO.

AA
AUTO ASSEMBLY.

AATON
A French manufacturer of film cameras.

A 2
Antenne 2, the second French state TV broadcasting
NETWORK.

A34
A DIGITAL integrated VIDEO production system from
ABEKAS, consisting of AUDIO and VIDEO mixers,
DVE and edit controller. Also known as SOLO.

A53D
A DVE from ABEKAS.

A60–A66
A family of random access COMPONENT DIGITAL
VIDEO DISK recorders from ABEKAS.

A72
A DIGITAL CHARACTER GENERATOR from
ABEKAS.

A84
A DIGITAL COMPONENT post production VISION
MIXER from ABEKAS.

A/B
As Before, a script abbreviation.

A/B ROLL WORKING
Film —
A method of assembling film sequences together from two rolls of film images which have SPACING or BLANKING on one roll, the 'A' roll, where images appear on the 'B' roll, and vice-versa. By having a slight overlap of material in each section, the transitions between sections can be WIPES or MIXES or other effects which require simultaneous contributions from two images.
Videotape —
The material to be edited on to the MASTER tape is sourced from two tapes, the A & B rolls. This allows image transitions other than cuts to be achieved. In some situations the B roll is a duplicate of the A roll.

ABC
1. The American Broadcasting Company, one of the major American TV networks.
2. The Australian Broadcasting Commission.

ABEKAS
A manufacturer of broadcast DIGITAL television systems. Generally refers to the A53D three dimensional DIGITAL VIDEO EFFECTS system used in studios and post production.

ABOVE THE LINE
The variable creative programme costs for which PRODUCERS are responsible in their budget.

ABS
Association of Broadcasting and allied Staffs, formerly one of the main trades unions representing staff at the BBC and the IBA transmitters, now merged with BETA.

AC
Alternating current, an electric current which changes polarity at regular intervals. Electricity power stations generate electric current at a frequency of 50 polarity changes per second in most of the world with the exception of the American continent where it is 60 polarity changes or cycles per second.

ACADEMY
The Academy of Motion Picture Arts and Sciences.

ACADEMY AWARD
Annual awards in the form of small gold plated statuettes awarded by the ACADEMY to artists and technicians for excellence in their field.

ACADEMY APERTURE
An opening, in a 35mm film camera or projector, of dimensions specified by the ACADEMY where 35mm film FRAMES are located for exposure or projection of the images.

ACADEMY LEADER
A standard 'run-in' film section designed by the ACADEMY, which is inserted at the beginning of a feature film or release print. It contains a visual countdown sequence and audible soundtrack cueing information.

ACE
A computerised videotape edit controller manufactured by the AMPEX corporation — Ampex Computerised Editing.

ACMADE
The proprietary name of a film editing machine consisting of sprocketed wheels for the transport of the film and associated sound tracks. A small ground glass screen is used to view the image, and a small loudspeaker is used to monitor the sound.

ACQUIRED PROGRAMME
Programme material which has been purchased rather than produced by the end user.

ACR
Automatic Cassette Recorder. A QUADRUPLEX
videotape recorder, using 2" wide videotape that can
play 24 CASSETTES of up to 6 mins. duration in any
order, from an instant start. Used primarily for the
transmission of COMMERCIAL and PROMOTION
SPOTS.

ACTION
The command from a DIRECTOR to artists to
commence their performance.

ACTION REPLAY
The replaying of a recorded highlight from a televised
sporting event immediately after the event has
occurred. Used for analysis by a commentator or
viewer.

ACTT
The Association of Cinematograph, Television and
allied Technicians. One of the main trades unions of
the film and television companies, now merged with
BETA to form BECTU.

A/D
ANALOGUE to DIGITAL.

ADA
Audio distribution amplifier — an AUDIO amplifier that
receives one input and delivers several identical
outputs to various destinations in a facility.

ADAC
Advanced DIGITAL Adaptive Converter. A high quality
broadcast TV STANDARDS converter manufactured by
ABS.

ADLOG
An electronic system which automatically logs the
transmission of a COMMERCIAL by decoding DIGITAL
information inserted in the VERTICAL INTERVAL by
the producing company.

ADO
Ampex Digital Optics. A DVE from AMPEX.

ADR
Automatic Dialogue Replacement, the post production process of adding dialogue to a film section by artists viewing a continuous loop of film which shows the same scene repeatedly. This allows artists several attempts at matching their voice to their filmed lip movements.

ADS
Advanced Digital Scanner. The proprietary name of Rank Cintel for a SOLID STATE film scanning device for a TELECINE machine which uses a CCD image transducer.

AES
AUDIO Engineering Society (USA).

AES/EBU INTERCONNECT
A universally accepted specification laid down by the AES and EBU for the conversion of a dual channel ANALOGUE sound signal into a serial DIGITAL format which can be carried over normal audio cables and connectors.

AF
AUDIO Frequency. The frequency spectrum sensed by the human ear as sound. It varies with the individual, but generally accepted as being between 20 and 20,000 Hz.

AFL
(Affle) After Fader Listen. The ability to listen to one or more sources on a sound mixing desk without affecting the FINAL MIX.

AFM
An AUDIO signal recorded on a videotape recorder by means of FREQUENCY MODULATION.

AFTERGLOW
The decaying emission of light from a CRT after the electron beam has been cut off.

AFV
AUDIO Follows VIDEO. A mode of operation of a VISION MIXER or video routing matrix in which a sound mixer or sound routing matrix mimics the vision source selected.

AGB
Audits of Great Britain — an audience research organisation.

AKG
Akutische und Kino Gerate — Sound and Film Equipment (German). An Austrian manufacturer of professional sound equipment, renowned for its microphones.

ALL
A transmission RUNNING ORDER note to indicate that every broadcaster on a NETWORK is to transmit the indicated programme.

ALEX
An advanced DIGITAL CHARACTER GENERATOR manufactured by the AMPEX corporation which allows dynamic manipulation of individual characters.

ALIAS, ALIASING
The generation of spurious image information in a system where the image sampling rate is too low with respect to the rate of change of image content.
A good example of this phenomenon occurs when a spoked wheel appears to rotate in the opposite direction to its actual direction when viewed on film, the sampling rate of the film camera shutter of 24 FPS being less than twice the rate of wheel rotation.
In DIGITAL systems, aliasing causes stepped ragged edges on the sloping lines of characters due to the smallest PIXEL being a well defined square and not a soft edged ellipse as generated by an ANALOGUE camera pick - up tube.

AM
Amplitude Modulation. The process of conveying an
ANALOGUE signal by varying the amplitude of a fixed
high frequency 'carrying signal' in sympathy with the
signal being conveyed.

AMIGO
The proprietary name of RANK CINTEL for an
electronic film preprogramming system that stores
information relating to the exposure, colour,
magnification and position of a film image on a shot by
shot basis for later recall. Operates in conjunction with
the Mk3 TELECINE.

AMPEX
An American manufacturer of television equipment,
specifically VTRs and videotape, named after its
founder Alexander M. Ponatoff and the first two letters
of the word EXcellence.

AMS
Advanced Music Systems — the manufacturer of the
AUDIOFILE DIGITAL AUDIO EDITOR.

ANALOGUE
A continuously varying signal proportional to a change
in image or sound information.

ANAMORPHIC LENS
An optical lens that has different magnification factors
in the horizontal and vertical planes. *See*
CINEMASCOPE.

ANCHOR
The main presenter of a programme involving several
contributors.

ANGENIEUX
A French manufacturer of optical products especially
lenses for (TV) cameras.

ANG
ANGLIA TV

ANGLIA TV
The independent commercial TV company serving the east of England with headquarters in Norwich.

ANIMATION
The generation of moving graphics or models by running a sequence of still images of the subject, each image showing the subject in a slightly different position.

ANN
Announcer, a script abbreviation. The person who provides continuity at programme junctions.

ANNT
Announcement, a script abbreviation.

A&R
Artists and Repertoire, the department or individual of a recording company concerned with the promotion and development of an artist.

'A' ROLL
One of a pair of film or videotape reels, the other being the 'B' roll.

ANSWER PRINT
The first GRADED print from an edited NEGATIVE colour film sent from the processing laboratory for approval by the customer.

ANTI-ALIASED
The removal of the 'stairstepping' on the sloping edges of DIGITALLY generated text characters by sophisticated computer SOFTWARE techniques.

AP
Associated Press, an international news agency.

APL
Average Picture Level — the signal level or grey tone which repesents the average in a video image.

APERTURE
The adjustable opening in a lens system that regulates the transmission of light through it.

APERTURE CORRECTION
The process of boosting the high frequencies in the VIDEO circuits of TV image generating equipment to improve apparent image detail.

APPLE
An American computer company which developed the 'MACintosh' family of personal computers.

APPLE BOX
Wooden boxes which are used to raise an artist or a PROP above studio floor level to improve the composition of a shot.

APRON
The part of a theatrical stage in front of the curtain.

APRS
The Association of Professional Recording Studios.

ARCHIVE
Long term store for film and videotapes etc.

ARD
The first German TV NETWORK.

ARRI
Arnold and Richter — a German manufacturer of film cameras and lighting equipment.

ARTEFACT
An unwanted visible product generated in a video system due to some technical shortcoming. *See* FOOTPRINT, MOIRE.

ARTFILE
A DIGITAL picture store with added graphic and PAINTING facilities. Operated by means of an artist's tablet and magnetic pen in conjunction with MENUS displayed on a TV MONITOR screen.

ARTWORK
Any printed, drawn or painted material on paper or card.

ASA
American Standards Authority. Noted for its standard relating to the light sensitivity of photographic film emulsion (eg 100 ASA). The higher the number, the more sensitive the film is to light.

ASCII
American Standard Code for Information Interchange. A computer data coding system for the transmission of alphanumeric and control characters.

ASIC
Application Specific Integrated Circuit. An INTEGRATED CIRCUIT designed specifically for a purpose. This results in an electronic system with very few peripheral components and a consequent reduction in size and failure rate.

'A' SIDE
The most commercially successful side of a SINGLE.

ASM
Assistant Stage Manager. A member of a drama production team on the studio floor, who prompts artists when they forget their lines. They are also charged with maintaining continuity and the wellbeing of the artists.

ASPECT RATIO
The ratio of picture width to picture height. The TV screen has an aspect ratio of 4x3, or 1.33:1

ASSEMBLE EDIT
In videotape editing, an assemble edit is one in which new VIDEO images and/or sound, CONTROL TRACK and TIMECODE are sequentially added to the previous material on the tape.

ASSOCIATE PRODUCER
An assistant producer with some specialist knowledge or input to the subject of a programme.

AST
Automatic Scan Tracking — the proprietary name of a
system developed by the AMPEX corporation which
allows the video playback head of a HELICAL format
VTR to accurately follow the recorded video tracks at
differing linear tape speeds thus allowing the
generation of broadcast quality videotape pictures at
variable speeds including stop.

ASTON
The proprietary name of an electronic DIGITAL
CHARACTER GENERATOR used for the production of
CAPTIONS, CRAWLS, ROLLERS OR LOGOS.

ASTRA
A pan-European extraterrestrial communications
satellite for DBS use.

AT
Advanced Technology, a PC based on the Intel 80286
16 BIT processor which operates quicker than the XT.

ATC
Assistant Transmission Controller. The person in an
MCR who operates the various equipment to ensure a
continuous feed of vision and sound from a studio
centre to the transmitters.

ATR
AUDIO Tape Recorder.

ATMOS
Atmosphere, background ambient sounds.

ATTENUATOR
An electronic device which is used to reduce the value
of an electrical signal.

AUDIO
The sound or dialogue in a production.

AUDIOFILE
The proprietary name of a device which is used for the
storage and editing of AUDIO in DIGITAL form, using a
WINCHESTER DISK as the data storage medium.

AUTO ASSEMBLY

The editing together of videotaped programme sections under computer control from a previously entered edit decision list. Edit controllers can assemble the material by one of two methods:

A mode — the editing computer reads the edit list in ascending event number order, ie it replicates the OFF-LINE edit.

B mode — the editing computer plays back material from the currently mounted reels, recording the material on the

master tape in the correct position and leaving gaps for the material from subsequently mounted source reels.

B mode can be quicker than an A mode assembly as the source reels only move in a forward direction to present the next piece of material for an edit, leaving the master tape to spool to the next edit position from either direction.

AUTOCLEAN

A computer programme that CLEANS an edit list as it is generated during an edit session.

AUTO CONFORMING

The editing together of videotaped programme sections under computer control, from an edit decision list previously generated on low cost OFF-LINE equipment.

The three types of CLEANED edit lists used are:

A mode — the material is recorded on to the master tape in edit list order; this is generally programme order except for DROP INS or CUTAWAYS which over - record previous material.

B mode — the edit list is reorganised such that no recorded material is over - recorded to produce the final composite edit thus speeding up the process.

C mode — the edit list is the same as a B mode list but with the edit events arranged in ascending TIMECODE and source reel number thus reducing the number of reel changes.

AUTOCUE
The proprietary name for a device that projects a rolling
script on to an angled semi-silvered mirror positioned in
front of the camera lens, so that a presenter looks at
the camera lens whilst reading the script. The speed of
the roller is controlled by the autocue operator who also
generates and alters the text during preparation of the
programme. Some newscasters control the roller speed
from a nearby control.

AUTOSCORE
An enhancement to QUANTEL's CYPHER which
allows the dynamic updating of designed graphical
characters from the inputting of alphanumeric data from
a computer keyboard.

AUTOSCRIPT
A computer based script prompter that can be
interfaced to the BAYSYS newsroom electronic
publishing system.

AV
Audio Visual, generally used to describe live
presentations by the use of transparency slides
accompanied by prerecorded dialogue or music.

AWB
Auto WHITE BALANCE.

A WIND
A videotape wound on a reel in a clockwise direction
with the OXIDE on the inside.

AXE
To halt the production of a programme or terminate a
series before its scheduled conclusion.

AZIMUTH
The angle of the gap in a magnetic or optical
transducer with respect to the dirction of tape or film
motion.

B
Blue, one of the three primary colours used to produce the colour spectrum in a TV system.

B&B
Black and Burst, a VIDEO signal which contains all the requisite synchronising information but no image information.

BBC
The British Broadcasting Corporation.

BABY
A small spotlight.

BABY LEGS
A small camera tripod used for LOW ANGLE shots.

BABY SPOT
A small spotlight containing a 500–750 watt lamp which is used to illuminate part of a subject.

BACKCLOTH
A large scenic background for a studio SET, usually painted on a canvas or CYC.

BACK FOCUS
The distance between the rear element of a ZOOM lens and the image transducer in a camera, it is adjusted to give a sharp image when the lens is set at its widest taking angle.

BACKLIGHT
One of the three classical modelling lights used to illuminate a subject. It is used to light the subject from behind and has the effect of enhancing the subject's outline thereby lifting the subject from its background and imparting depth to the scene.

BACK PORCH
The back porch of a COMPOSITE VIDEO signal is the short period between the trailing edge of the LINE SYNC pulse and the beginning of active video.

BACK PROJECTION
A method of providing scenic settings, mostly of a secondary nature, by projecting them from film or slides onto the back of a translucent screen.

BACKING
1. The section of a studio SET usually seen through a door or window.
2. Theatrical DRAPES behind a performer.

BACKING TRACK
Sound, usually recorded music, used to accompany a vocal or added at the DUBBING stage to a film.

BACK REF
To make reference to a news story or item that has just occurred.

BACKSTAGE
The areas of a theatrical stage behind and to the side of the performing area which are not seen by the audience.

BACK TIME
The process of timing a section of programme material from an end point backwards into the material to establish a start point that allows the end point to occur at a specific time.

BACK TO BACK
A cable plug sex changer, *see* MALE, FEMALE and GENDER BENDER.

BACKTRACK
SOFTWARE in a computerised OFF-LINE edit system which traces back from a final edit list, which may contain several SUB MASTERS or sub-sub masters and locates the first GENERATION playback tapes and TIMECODES for use in an AUTO ASSEMBLY in order to ensure optimum picture quality.

BAFTA
British Academy of Film and Television Arts.

BALANCE
1. The adjusting of the various sound levels on a sound mixing desk to give a pleasing homogeneous result.
2. The adjusting of the Red, Green and Blue colour signals of a TV camera to produce a neutral, (balanced) scale of tones from black to white whilst viewing a monochrome test chart; a prerequisite to producing a faithful colour TV picture.
3. The adjusting of the various LUMINAIRES in a lighting SET-UP to produce the desired effect whilst remaining within the contrast ratio acceptable by the medium.

BALANCE STRIPE
A thin stripe of magnetic oxide on the opposite edge of 16mm film stock to the sound track which ensures uniform winding on a reel.

BALL AND BISCUIT
An omnidirectional moving coil microphone in the shape of a ball surmounted by a disc windshield.

BANDWIDTH
The range of signal frequencies that a device or system can usefully handle.

BANKING
General library material or recorded studio sketches which are stockpiled for use in a programme which contains an element of topical material. The material is usually non topical and can be used at any time when there is a shortfall of interesting topical material.

BANTAM JACK
A miniature P.O. type JACKPLUG.

BARB
Broadcasting Audience Research Board. An agency which provides statistical analysis of the viewing public based on a cross sample of approximately 4000 homes.

BARN DOOR
Folding metal flaps on studio lamps used to shield or direct light.

BARNEY
A cover put over a film camera to reduce its mechanical noise whilst sound filming.

BARRACUDA
A telescopic support for a LUMINAIRE which hangs from a lighting grid.

BARREL
1. A VIDEO cable connector that joins two cables together.
2. A studio lighting support capable of supporting groups of LUMINAIRES.

BASE
1. A TV studio centre.
2. A prearranged rendezvous for a location shoot.
3. The flexible medium which carries the light sensitive emulsion of a film or the magnetic oxide of magnetic recording tape.

BASEBAND
The frequency spectrum of a signal before entering a modulation system for conversion to a higher frequency spectrum for processing or transmission.

BASHER
A simple lamp in a dished reflector placed near the camera on a stand or attached to the camera for local supplementary illumination.

BAUD
The unit of speed of digital data transmission. Named after French engineer J.M.E. BAUDot.

BAYSYS
A computerised newsroom publishing system for use in the TV broadcasting environment.

BAZOOKA
A camera mounting in the form of an adjustable monopod for use in restricted locations.

B & C
Blacked & Coded, a videotape on which CONTROL TRACK, TIMECODE and COLOUR BLACK signals have been recorded as a prerequisite to INSERT editing.

BCC
Broadcasting Complaints Commission.

BCU
Big Close Up, a camera shot that is so close as to reveal only part of the whole subject in the picture frame, eg in relation to a person, this would be the face or part of the face.

BDR
BORDER TELEVISION

BEARDING
The ragging or tearing between horizontally adjacent light and dark areas of a TV picture caused by exceeding the electronic design limits of the television system.

BEAT
A short pause in dialogue.

BECTU
The Broadcasting, Entertainment, Cinema and Theatre Union, formed from the amalgamation of ACTT and BETA.

BED
Bedrock, the musical or visual foundation upon which an edited piece is constructed.

BEEB
The British Broadcasting Corporation.

BELOW THE LINE
Internal programme technical servicing costs.

BEST BOY
An assistant to the GAFFER or KEY GRIP in a film or video production.

BETA
Broadcasting and Entertainment Trades Alliance.

BETACAM
The proprietary name of the SONY Corporation for a cassette based COMPONENT VTR format which uses 1/2" wide video tape. Some specially designed VTRs can be mounted inside the video cameras. (Camcorder)

BETACAM SP
BETACAM **S**uperior **P**erformance
The proprietary name for an enhanced version of BETACAM which uses metal particle tape and different recording characteristics to produce improved images and two HI-FI FM sound tracks in addition to the two ANALOGUE tracks on BETACAM.

BETACART
Proprietary name for a computer controlled multi - CASSETTE video player using the BETACAM format.

BETAMAX
A domestic videocassette format developed by SONY to compete with the VHS format.

BFBS
British Forces Broadcasting Service.

BFI
British Film Institute.

B FORMAT
A 1" HELICAL VTR standard developed by BOSCH. It requires two revolutions of the video HEAD DRUM to record one TV FIELD, consequently, a FRAME store is required for slow motion and freeze frames.

B/G
Background, a script abbreviation.

BH
Broadcasting House, a BEEB term for the headquarters of BBC radio in London and the regional radio and TV broadcasting centres.

BIAS
1.   A high frequency AC signal used in audio tape recorders to minimise distortion of the recorded signal caused by the non-linear transfer characteristic of magnetic tape.
2.   A small light source used to illuminate the target of a TV camera pick-up tube to minimise the effects of LAG and SMEAR on low light level shots.
3.   Prejudice by a member of a programme production team or presenter which inhibits impartiality or balanced argument.

BIOPIC
A portmanteau word for a filmed biography.

BIN
A cloth lined receptacle for holding lengths of unwound film during editing.

BINARY DIGIT
The digits 0 or 1, which are used in DIGITAL computing systems and represent two states, present or not present , on or off .

BIRD
An extraterrestrial communications satellite.

BIT
A BINARY DIGIT.

BITC
Burnt In TimeCode. TIMECODE numbers which appear
in the related picture for logging purposes and
subsequent editing.

BIT PART
A performer whose contribution is of minor significance.

BKSTS
British Kinematograph, Sound and Television Society.

BLACK CRUSHED
The loss of detail in the dark areas of a TV image by
reducing the signal that specifies the dark tones to
BLACK LEVEL.

BLACKED
1. A 'BLACKED' videotape is one on which COLOUR
BLACK,CONTROL TRACK PULSES AND TIMECODE
have been recorded as a prerequisite for INSERT
EDITING.
2. Any programme material which has been
'embargoed' by a trades union.

BLACK LEVEL
The minimal voltage of the picture signal that ensures
the blackness of the transmitted picture.

BLACKS
Black cloth drapes or black painted FLATS used in a
studio to produce no picture detail in certain areas of a
scene.

BLACK SLUG
Black spacing and silence inserted between parts of a
videotaped programme to ensure that consecutive
parts appear at the correct time when the programme is
played from the beginning without being stopped and
restarted between commercial breaks. Used
extensively in the USA.

BLANK
An unvoiced PROMO or TRAIL without
SUPERIMPOSED CAPTIONS which is played out on a
NETWORK for the use of other broadcasters.

BLANKING
That part of the VIDEO signal during which the image information is cut off to permit the invisible retrace of the scanning electron beam in a CRT or image transducer from the end of one line to the beginning of the next, and from the bottom of one FIELD to the top of the next. It forms a black frame around the TV image and contains the 'blacker than black' SYNCHRONISING pulses which enable the serially transmitted VIDEO to be reconstructed back into the image being televised.

BLEACHERS
Extendible ranks of audience seating used in a studio — derived from the unroofed seating at American sports grounds which are constantly bleached by exposure to the sun.

BLIMP
A rigid soundproofed housing for a film camera which has the camera controls extended to the outside.

BLIND EDIT
See INVISIBLE EDIT.

BLOCK BOOKING
The booking of technical facilities by a production for the entire duration of its run in order to ensure their availability.

BLONDE
A proprietary name for a 2 KW variable focus lamp.

BNC
Bayonet Nut Connector or Bayonet Neill Concelman (U.S. designer), a twist lock VIDEO cable connector.

BOF
Bottom Of (picture) Frame.

BOP
Beginning Of (programme) Part.

BOOM
A wheeled trolley with a horizontal telescopic arm for the placing and directing of a microphone.

BOOT
Bootstrap, a short sequence of commands which are
carried out to start up a computer, either from a switch
on (cold start) or from a system reset (warm start).

BORDER
The ITV franchise holder covering the area around the
English Scottish border.

BOTTOM HALF
A lamp diffuser which is placed over the bottom half of
a studio lamp to modify the light output.
See YASHMAK.

BOUNCE
The process of playing AUDIO from one track of a
MULTITRACK ATR or VTR and simultaneously re -
recording that track with some modification onto
another track.

BOX
1. 'In the' — studio control room.
2. 'On the' — on television.

BOX SET
A studio SET which has four walls, one of which has to
be removed in turn for camera access.

BPI
British Phonographic Industry.

BREATHING
1. Variations in focus of a projected film caused by
movement of the film in and out of the focal plane in
either the camera or projector.
2. Variations in focus of a TV picture due to
irregularities of the supply voltage used to focus the
electron beam in either the TV camera or TV monitor.

BREEZEWAY
That part of the COMPOSITE VIDEO signal between
the trailing edge of the LINE SYNCHRONISING pulse
and the beginning of the COLOUR BURST.

BRIDGING SHOT
A camera shot that is used to disguise any disruption in place or time continuity of a scene.

'B' ROLL
1. In the film environment, a reel of film image sections separated by BLANKING where images appear on the 'A' ROLL.
2. In the videotape editing environment, a duplicate of original material to allow mixing and effects between shots.

BROWSE
The attribute of a STILL STORE that allows the viewing of multiple reduced size images simultaneously in numerical order, as an aid to identifying and locating material.

BRT
Belgische Radio en Televisie, the Belgian state broadcaster which broadcasts in the Flemish language.

BRUTE
A very large carbon arc lamp.

BSB
A DBS franchise holder transmitting exclusively to the UK using DMAC technology.

'B' SIDE
The less commercial side of a SINGLE.

BSKYB
British Sky Broadcasting. The satellite TV broadcasting company formed by the merger of BSB and SKY television which broadcasts to the UK and Europe using the PAL TV system.

BT
British Telecom. A self governing body which is responsible for communications in the UK.

BT LINES
Sound and vision cables from a facility into the British Telecom communication NETWORK.

BTS
Broadcast Television Systems. The company formed by the merger of certain sections of PHILIPS INDUSTRIES of Holland and THE BOSCH GROUP of Germany for the design and marketing of broadcast hardware.

BUBBLE
The generic name for an incandescent light bulb in a studio lamp.

BULK ERASER
A device used to rapidly erase magnetic tapes without the need to unwind the tape from its reel.

BUG
A computer programme error which produces erroneous results in a system. In extreme cases can cause the system to cease operating.

BUMP
The process of altering the linear tape speed of a VTR a preset number of FRAMES at a time whilst the tape is in motion. This is sometimes used to synchronise one VTR with another, by listening to the sound playback from both VTRs simultaneously, AUDIO SYNC and hence picture sync can be achieved.

BUMPER
A 5 second ANIMATION or LOGO which is used to separate a programme from the COMMERCIALS.

BURN
1. Damage to a camera pick-up tube due to prolonged exposure to a bright subject, a faint image of the subject remaining visible long after the subject matter has changed.
2. Damage to the light producing phosphors on a CRT face due to the prolonged displaying of bright static images. This causes a ghost of the image to remain on the tube face.

BURNT IN
1. Alphanumeric characters permanently added to
programme material for logging purposes in a viewing
tape.
2. LOGOS permanently added to broadcast programme
material for source identification and copyright
purposes, especially from a broadcast satellite.

BURNT OUT
Loss of definition in the highlights of a picture due to
over exposure of a camera or TELECINE.

BURST
That portion of the COMPOSITE colour video signal
which consists of 10 cycles of colour SUBCARRIER
inserted in LINE BLANKING between the trailing edge
of the LINE SYNC pulse and the beginning of ACTIVE
VIDEO.

BUS (BUSS)
1. A row of pushbuttons on a VISION MIXER control
panel which allows any of a number of picture sources
to appear on the output.
2. A data signal path inside a computer consisting of 8
parallel routes, or multiples thereof.

BUSK
To proceed without any rehearsal.

BUY THAT!
An indication from the DIRECTOR of a good TAKE.

BUZZ TRACK
1. A special test film for checking the alignment of the
optical sound pick-up head on a TELECINE machine.
2. Atmospheric background sounds recorded for later
use in POST PRODUCTION.

BVB
Black Video Black, a videotape editing preview mode
that displays black, the newly inserted VIDEO and
black again. Very useful for determining FRAME
accurate in and out edit points.

BVH
Broadcast Video Helical scan. SONY term for a C
FORMAT reel to reel COMPOSITE VIDEO, HELICAL
VTR using 1" wide videotape.

BVU
Broadcast Video U-Matic. SONY term for
COMPOSITE VIDEO, HELICAL VIDEOCASSETTE
recorder using 3/4" wide videotape, known as
U-MATIC.

BVW
SONY term for HELICAL, ANALOGUE COMPONENT,
VIDEOCASSETTE recorder using 1/2" wide videotape,
known as BETACAM.

B/W
Black and White, a script abbreviation.

B WIND
Videotape wound on a reel OXIDE out.

B-Y
One of the two CHROMINANCE signals generated in
an ENCODED colour television system, formed by
subtracting the brightness signal (Y) from the blue
signal (B). Producing a CHROMINANCE signal in this
manner ensures that no brightness information is
carried by the CHROMINANCE signal and the
CHROMINANCE signal is zero when a
MONOCHROME picture is transmitted.

BYTE
A group of BITS in a DIGITAL system.

C
Centrestage, a script abbreviation.

CABLE BASHER
An assistant studio cameraman whose job is to pay out and control the cable that connects a studio TV camera to a socket on the studio wall.

CALL SHEET
A chronological list of a performer's appointments with the various service departments (eg make-up, wardrobe, etc.) in a studio centre or location.

CAM
Camera, a script abbreviation.

CAM L
Camera left, a script abbreviation.

CAM R
Camera right, a script abbreviation.

CAMCORDER
A lightweight hand held TV camera that contains an inbuilt VIDEOCASSETTE recorder.

CAMERA CARD
Cards, one for each camera, prepared in advance of the CR by the PA, which contain a list of each camera operator's camera shots and movements.

CAM REMOTE
The proprietary name of a remote controlled pan and tilt head for film and video cameras, usually attached to the end of a boom arm.

CAMERA SCRIPT
The document that contains the script and technical instructions for all concerned in a production.

CAMERA TAPE
A fabric based general purpose adhesive tape which is used to secure anything to anything.

CAN
In the can - filming or recording (video) is completed.

CANDELA
A reference standard candle of specified intensity.

CANNON
A manufacturer of cable plugs and sockets, specifically the three pin audio cable connector used by broadcasting professionals.
See XLR.

CANS
Headphones worn by various members of a TV studio crew in order to receive instruction from the GALLERY.

CAP
CAPTION, a script abbreviation.

CAPGEN
The proprietary name of an electronic CAPTION generator manufactured by RYLEY COMMUNICATIONS.

CAPSTAN
The rotating spindle on a tape deck which moves the tape at a linear speed past the recording heads.

CAPTAIN
Commissioning, Acquisition, Programme Transmission and Information Network. A computer system used in conjunction with CATS which enables a high level of automation in CHANNEL FOUR's television operations.

CAPTION
1. A still picture, or card containing printed matter.
2. A proprietary name of electronic TV character generator developed by ASTON Electronics.

CAPTION SCANNER
A device that scans a CAPTION card to produce a TV image.

CAP UP
The process of placing a protective cover over a camera lens after use. Most TV cameras also allow the insertion of an opaque disk between the rear element of a camera lens system and the pick up tube. This prevents possible damage to the tube when leaving the camera trained on a bright subject for a considerable time.

CAR
Central Apparatus Room, the main equipment area of a TV station or facility.

CARDIOID MICROPHONE
A microphone which has a heart shaped response field.

CARLTON
The London based facilities company that secured the ITV weekday franchise for the London area in October 1991.

CARNET
An inventory of equipment used on an overseas assignment which is required for customs clearance.

CAROUSEL
An enhancement to QUANTEL'S PAINTBOX which allows the storage of up to 12 seconds of video still FRAMES in such a manner that they can be rapidly recalled in a sequence to produce an animated or moving image.

CART
Cartridge, a case that contains an endless loop of audio tape on one reel.

CASSETTE
A protective case which contains magnetic tape on a supply reel which is received by the take-up reel after the tape has passed through the recording/playing device.

CATCHLIGHT
The specular reflection of a light source in a performer's eye.

CATS(WHISKER)
A small movement of a camera or PROP.

CATS
Computer Assisted Transmission system. A computer driven automated TV transmission system used by CH4 and others.

CATWALK
An overhead walkway in a studio for gaining access to the LIGHTING GRID.

CAV
Component Analogue Video. A video system in which the LUMINANCE and CHROMINANCE signals of a TV image are kept separate and whose magnitudes are represented by a varying voltage.

CB
1. Commercial Break, a script abbreviation.
2. The 'scaled down' or weighted (B-Y) COLOUR DIFFERENCE signal in a COMPONENT ANALOGUE VIDEO signal.

CBS
Columbia Broadcasting System, one of the three major American TV NETWORKS.

CCD
Charge Coupled Device. A microchip in a TV camera or TELECINE machine that converts a light image on its surface into a VIDEO signal.

CCIR
Comité Consultative International des Radio communications (FRENCH). International radio consultative committee — a regulatory body concerned with the formulation of radio and TV standards and recommendations.

CCIR 601
An internationally agreed standard specifying the conversion of COMPONENT VIDEO signals into DIGITAL data.

CCIR 656
An internationally agreed standard specifying the electromechanical interfacing of equipment which conforms to the '601' standard.

CCU
Camera Control Unit. The part of a TV camera system which contains the majority of the electronics and allows the remote control of many of the camera functions.

CD
Compact Disc. An AUDIO medium in which a rotating silvered disc is scanned by a laser beam and the resulting DIGITAL information converted into sound.

CEEFAX
The TELETEXT information system designed and used by the BBC. (See Facts!)

CEL
A single layer of celluloid with location holes onto which images are painted. The cels are then photgraphed to form an animation sequence.

CEN
CENTRAL.

CENTEXT
The in house TELETEXT information service of CENTRAL ITV.

CENTRAL
Central Indepenent Television, the independent
commercial television broadcaster which serves the
midlands area of England.

CENTRAL AREA
A technical equipment area which contains the
equipment for all aspects of transmission.

CENTRE TRACK
An audio recording along the middle of sprocketed
magnetic tape.

C FORMAT
The 1" COMPOSITE VIDEO, HELICAL VTR reel to
reel standard used by most broadcasting organisations.
One revolution of the video HEAD DRUM records one
TV FIELD.

CG
CAPTION Generator

CHA
CHANNEL

CHANNEL
The independent commercial television broadcaster
serving the Channel Islands.

CHARACTER GENERATOR
A computer based device that produces text on a TV
screen.

CHARISMA
A DVE by QUESTECH.

CHEAT
A small movement of something or somebody which is
spoiling the composition of a camera shot. This may
affect continuity but is sometimes necessary.

CHERRY PICKER
A lorry mounted hydraulic platform for raising cameras
or radio link equipment above ground.

CHINAGRAPH
A special coloured wax crayon for marking editing instructions on film.

CHINESE
A term used to describe the act of restricting the light from a LUMINAIRE by closing the top and bottom BARN DOORS such that a narrow horizontal slit is produced.

CHIP
An abbreviation for microchip which is jargon for microcircuit, an electronic circuit etched on a tiny piece of silicon and enclosed in plastic or ceramic casing.

CHIP CAMERA
A video camera which uses a CCD MICROCHIP as an optical transducer.

CHIP CHART
A camera greyscale test chart composed of accurately manufactured card rectangles of differing tones from black to white.

CHIPPY
A joiner who constructs studio scenery.

CHOP
To discontinue a programme during its production.

CHROMA
An abbreviation for CHROMINANCE, the colour portion of a television signal which contains the HUE and SATURATION information.

CHROMA KEY
A video effect in which parts of one TV image are replaced by another image, the area of image replacement being defined by a specific colour in the main image. Also known as COLOUR SEPARATION OVERLAY (CSO).

CHROMINANCE
The signal that contains the information pertaining to the HUE and SATURATION of a colour TV image.

CHYRON
An American manufacturer of DIGITAL TV equipment, known for its character generators.

CINCHING
'Accordion pleating', crease damage to tape caused by interlayer slippage on a spool due to incorrect tape tension.

CINEMAC
A method of archiving colour TV programmes on MONOCHROME film stock using MAC technology developed by Thames Television.

CINEMASCOPE
The proprietary name of 20TH CENTURY FOX for a motion picture film system in which a wide screen image of ASPECT RATIO 1:2.35 is formed from a standard ASPECT RATIO 35mm film FRAME by the use of an ANAMORPHIC lens in the camera to compress the horizontal field of view into the available film width.
 A complementary lens on the film projector expands the film image horizontally such that the wide screen aspect ratio is reformed.

CINERAMA
A motion picture system using three synchronised cameras and projectors to produce an image on an extra wide screen composed of the three images positioned side by side. The image produced occupies the entire horizontal field of view of an observer and so adds an extra element of realism. The effect tends to be defeated by the two areas of vertical overlap of the contributing images being visible.

CLAPPER
A SLATE board with a hinged bar attached at the top. Used to produce a sound when the bar is brought into contact with the slate board whilst being filmed. Used to establish the sound to picture relationship in editing. (Known as the sync point).

CLAPPER LOADER
A member of a film crew charged with operating the
CLAPPER board for each TAKE of a scene, ensuring
correct audio synchronisation and identification of the
material. Other responsibilies include that of loading the
film camera with magazines containing RAW film stock
when required.

CLASH
A clash is said to occur when COMMERCIALS
advertising the same product or service are transmitted
in the same commercial break.
Similarly, to avoid the suggestion that a programme is
being sponsored by a product or service, an artist is not
allowed to appear in a commercial which occurs during
a programme in which they take part.

CLEANED LIST
A technically perfect edit decision list which has had all
but the final edit attempts removed.

CLEAN EFFECTS
General background sounds.

CLEAN FEED(SOUND)
The mixed output of a sound desk comprising all
sources except that of the recipient of the feed.

CLEAN(NETWORK)FEED
The output of a TV broadcaster on a TV NETWORK,
without its COMMERCIALS or STATION IDENT. This
simplifies the inserting of each broadcasters locally
generated COMMERCIALS.

CLEAN UP
An electronic process carried out on a DIGITALLY
captured image to remove interFIELD flicker and the
PAL FOOTPRINT.

CLICK TRACK
A soundtrack with metronome clicks to assist in
musical time keeping.

CLIP
1. To cut short by direction or editorial decisions.
2. A short film sequence.
3. A threshold level adjustment on a VISION MIXER to which a KEY source's LUMINANCE or CHROMINANCE attributes are compared. Any value above the clip level will insert the key fill source; any value below the clip level will inhibit the key fill source appearing in the final composite picture.

CLONE
A DIGITAL COMPONENT videotape copy of a DIGITAL COMPONENT MASTER recording.

CLOCK HOUR
The time between successive whole clock hours, used for calculating the allocation of COMMERCIAL air time.

CLOCK NUMBER
An arbitrary number applied to the VTR CLOCK of an ACQUIRED PROGRAMME (in the absence of a programme or production number) to ensure transmission of the correct item.

CLOCK TIME CODE
A real time DIGITAL timing signal used to identify individual VIDEO FRAMES on a videotape.

CLEO
Curvilinear Effects Option. An enhancement to the CHARISMA DVE which produces a vast repertoire of three dimensional curved solids which can be manipulated in three dimensional space.

CLOGGING
See HEAD CLOG.

CLT
Compagnie Luxembourgoise de Telediffusion. A Luxembourg based media group with controlling interests in radio and television stations.

CMCCR
Central Mobile Colour Control Room. The main
co-ordinating SCANNER of a large OB involving
several SCANNERS.

CMCR
Colour Mobile Control Room.

CNR
CONTROL LINE with no Ringers. A dedicated
telephone communication circuit without the necessary
telephone exchange equipment that generates the
signals required to ring the bells on normal domestic
telephones.

COAX
Coaxial Cable. Cable used to carry VIDEO and RF
signals. It consists of a central insulated conductor
surrounded by an outer braiding to act as an electronic
screen to minimise the pick-up of extraneous signals.

COBWEB GUN
A handheld device that generates artificial cobwebs for
scenic decoration by feeding a special rubber solution
into the airflow from a fan.

CODER
An abbreviation for ENCODER.

COFFIN
A rectangular studio lamp enclosure that contains many
lamps which is used to produce soft shadowless light.

COI
Central Office of information. A government sponsored
information organisation concerned with the production
of short information and safety films.

COLOUR BALANCE
The process of adjusting the Red, Green and Blue
video signals in a colour TV camera to produce a
colour free image when viewing a MONOCHROME test
chart.

COLOUR BARS
An electronically generated test signal in the form of eight coloured vertical stripes. It is used to check the integrity of the TV system path from the camera to the transmitter.

COLOUR BLACK
A VIDEO signal which contains all the requisite synchronising information but no image information.

COLOUR BURST
The name given to the colour synchronising signal which consists of a 'burst' of 10 cycles of SUBCARRIER inserted into the BACK PORCH of the COMPOSITE television signal.

COLOUR CORRECTION
1. Coloured optical filters used in film laboratories to correct colour film at the time of printing.
2. Electronic correction used during the transfer of film to videotape for transmission purposes.
3. Electronic correction used to correct COMPONENT videotaped pictures shot under less than favourable conditions.

COLOUR FRAMING
Due to the complex nature of the PAL colour TV signal, a four FRAME or (eight FIELD) sequence of the colour synchronising signals exists. This must be preserved to achieve disturbance free video edits.

COLOUR PROD
The trade mark or LOGO of a programme production company which appears on the end of all its productions. It also contains a copyright symbol and the year of production in Roman numerals which taxes the knowledge of some production staff.

COLOUR SEPARATION OVERLAY
A VIDEO effect where a specified colour is separated from a colour TV picture and used to generate an electronic signal which replaces that colour with a second picture. *See* CHROMA KEY.

COLOUR TEMPERATURE
A term used to describe the colour characteristic of a light source. A black surface has been defined as one which reflects no light. Therefore, if a black substance is heated it will give off light of a certain colour dependent on the temperature of its surface, from a dull cherry red to a bluish white. The colour of the light source is expressed in degrees Kelvin.

COMBINER
A device used to combine the outputs of two or more channels of DVE to allow complex VIDEO effects to be generated.

COMMAG (Combined Magnetic). Film which has the associated sound track recorded on a magnetic stripe next to the picture frame.

COMMERCIAL
Air time bought by advertising agencies on behalf of clients who wish to advertise their goods or services on a commercial radio or TV station.

COMMOPT (Combined Optical). Film which has the sound track recorded photographically next to the picture frame.

COMPONENT ANALOGUE VIDEO (CAV)
A video system where the LUMINANCE and CHROMINANCE component signals of a colour TV image are carried along separate signal paths and therefore do not interfere with each other to cause picture degradation, as in a COMPOSITE TV system.

COMPOSITE
A video system where all the signals that relate to a colour TV image (including the SYNCHRONISING PULSES), are encoded into one signal for ease of distribution and transmission.

COMPRESSION
A system whereby a sound source is made to sound louder than its peak value would indicate. Generally used on pop music and commercials.

COMPRESSOR
A device for reducing the dynamic range of an audio signal without imparting distortion.

CONFORMING
The editing together of film or videotaped sections following an assembly listing or edit decision list.

CONTINUITY
1. The linking together of progammes on air by the use of announcements.
2. The recording of the current status of a scene by means of notes or polaroid photographs to verify the dialogue, make up, costume and position of the performers in the scene. This information is extremely important when shooting scenes out of sequence.

CONTOURING
A DVE effect whereby the image is transformed into separate layers much like a relief map.

CONTOURS OUT OF GREEN
The apparent enhancement of resolution of images from a three tube (RGB) colour TV camera by extracting resolution detail from the Green channel.

CONTROL LINE
A dedicated private wire telephone line rented from BRITISH TELECOM to offer direct communication between TV studios and OB locations.

CONTROL TRACK
1. A signal recorded onto a videotape along with every FRAME of VIDEO to control longitudinal tape motion and allow recovery of the video in a structured manner analogous to electronic film PERFORATIONS.
2. A videotape that has had COLOUR BLACK VIDEO, TIMECODE and a CONTROL TRACK signal recorded along its length as a prerequisite for INSERT EDITING.

CONVERGENCE
The accurate superimposition of the separate Red, Green and Blue images of a colour TV or monitor screen to produce a full colour image.

COOKIE
Cuckaloris. A piece of opaque material placed in front of a lamp, with holes cut out to produce patterned lighting.

COPY
1. A duplicate of a videotape recorded programme with associated TIMECODE.
2. Generic term for the printed matter relating to a news story.

CORE
The plastic or wooden hub on which a film is sometimes wound.

CORPSE
A performer laughing uncontrollably during a scene or TAKE.

COVE
A concave moulding placed on the studio floor at the bottom of a CYC to provide a seamless transition from CYC to floor thereby producing an 'infinite horizon' when evenly lit.

CNN
Cable News Network, an American satellite news TV station.

CR/CAM REH
Camera Rehearsal, a full technical rehearsal for the benefit of all concerned in a production.

CR
The 'scaled down' or weighted (R-Y) COLOUR DIFFERENCE signal in a COMPONENT ANALOGUE VIDEO signal group.

CRAB
Sideways movement of a camera with respect to its field of view.

CRANE
A wheeled camera mounting where the camera is attached to a long arm which can be raised or lowered to offer a variety of camera angles.

CRAWL
A roller CAPTION, electronically generated or
otherwise, which moves horizontally across the screen.

CREDITS
A list of performers and production staff involved in a
production

CRI
A Colour Reversal Intermediate. A negative copy
produced using REVERSAL STOCK.

CRIB CARD
A large card with a performer's lines and prompts which
is held up at the side of the camera that is being
'worked'.

CROP
To remove unwanted edges of a TV image by camera
framing or electronically, using the functions of a
STILL STORE or WIPE generator of a VISION MIXER.

CROSS CUT
To cut between two cameras on a VISION MIXER, or
edit back and forth between two scenes on film or
video tape.

CROSS COLOUR
A deficiency of the COMPOSITE encoding of a video
signal, due to LUMINANCE signals generated by fine
detail of the subject matter (eg check patterned sports
jackets) being misinterpreted as CHROMINANCE
signals and generating spurious colours which appear
as a 'shimmer'.

CROSSFADE
1. To fade down one channel of an AUDIO MIXER
whilst fading up another channel.
2. In VIDEO terms, a cross fade is a mix or lap dissolve
between two video sources.

CROSSING THE LINE
The line is an imaginary one parallel to the plane of
action.To shoot from both sides of, or cross the line
during a scene leads to confusing eyelines and material
that is almost impossible to edit together.

CROSSTALK
Mutual interference between two AUDIO or VIDEO
signals.

CRUSHED BLACKS
Loss or disguising of unwanted detail in the dark areas
of a TV image by reducing the electronic signals that
specify the dark tones of the image to BLACK LEVEL.
Used as an operational adjustment on a TV camera.

CRT
Cathode Ray Tube. A display device for converting a
VIDEO signal into a visual image. Used in TV
receivers, picture and WAVEFORM MONITORS and
VDUs on computers.

CSA
Community Service Announcements, free air time for
worthy causes.

CSI
Compact Source Iodide . A type of high output lamp of
specified COLOUR TEMPERATURE.

CSO
Colour Separation Overlay. *See* CHROMA KEY.

CTE
Central Television Enterprises. The programme sales
and distribution subsidiary of Central Independent
Television.

CTDM
Compressed Time Division Multiplex. The process
used in the BETACAM VIDEOCASSETTE system
whereby the two CHROMINANCE signals are
squeezed to enable them to occupy the same track
length on the videotape as the adjacently recorded
LUMINANCE signal.
On playback, the CHROMINANCE signals are
unsqueezed in the TBC.

CTTC
CENTRE TRACK TIMECODE.

CU
Close up. A script abbreviation denoting a head and shoulders camera shot.

CUE (ACTION!)
The instruction from a DIRECTOR for performers to begin.

CUE CARDS
Large cards containing a performer's prompts or dialogue which are held up next to the camera that the performer is working to.

CUE DOT
1. A small black and white square inlaid in the top right corner of a video image (LIVE or recorded) one minute before the end of programme part to warn MCR and /or the other ITV contractors of an approaching COMMERCIAL break. It is extinguished 5 seconds before end of programme to act as a cue for MCR and/or the other contractors to roll their own commercials.
2. Small circular marks in the top right hand corner of a film frame to warn a projectionist of an imminent reel change from one projector to the other.

CUE TRACK
A low quality AUDIO TRACK on a VTR which is used to carry audio pips or voice for editing and cueing purposes.

CUT
1. Cessation of action in front of camera.
2. Instantaneous change of image or sound source.

CUTAWAY
Brief shot which 'cuts away' from the main action eg audience reaction to a performer.

CUT-OFF
That part of the active picture not seen on a domestic TV receiver.

CUTTER
1. A person who cuts the master negative into the programme sequences from the model produced by the film editor.
2. An upgradable, PC based videotape editing system which controls only two VT machines and hence can only carry out picture cuts.

CUT THROAT
A visual gesture from a FLOOR MANAGER to a presenter or performer to conclude immediately.

CUTTING COPY
The film print to which the editing is being performed. (also known as the work print.)

CUTTING ROOM
The film editor's work room.

CVS
Colour COMPOSITE VIDEO signal.

CVBS
Colour VIDEO BASEBAND Signal.

CYAN
The complementary colour to Red.

CYC (SIKE) CYCLORAMA.
A ceiling to floor tensioned curtain around the walls of a studio, used for the generation of uniform and illuminated backgrounds.

CYC TRACK
A studio fixture from which the CYC is hung.

CYPHER
A character generator which contains a DVE for the manipulation of the composed graphic.

D
DOWNSTAGE, a script abbreviation.

D/R
1. Dress Rehearsal/Dress Run. A rehearsal in full costume and make-up, generally the final rehearsal before transmission or a TAKE.
2. A Dispatch Rider.

D 1
A studio and post production DIGITAL COMPONENT VIDEOCASSETTE recording standard which uses 3/4" wide videotape. Its main advantage is the almost imperceptable GENERATION loss of the images when copied many times and the excellent image quality when used in CHROMA KEYING effects.

D 2
A studio and post production DIGITAL COMPOSITE VIDEOCASSETTE recording standard which uses 3/4" wide videotape. Its main advantage is that the GENERATION LOSS is less than 1" C FORMAT ANALOGUE VTR and it is cheaper than D1 to purchase and operate.

D 3
A DIGITAL COMPOSITE acquisition and recording VIDEOCASSETTE standard developed by Panasonic using 1/2" wide videotape with all the generation loss benefits of D2.

D 5
A DIGITAL COMPONENT acquisition and recording VIDEOCASSETTE standard developed by Panasonic using 1/2" wide videotape with all the generation loss benefits of D1.

DA
Distribution Amplifier, an amplifier that accepts a single input and produces multiple identical outputs for distribution in a system.

DAILIES
Prompt, dirty, and generally ungraded prints of a day's shooting. *See* RUSHES.

DAR
DIGITAL AUDIO Recording.

DARK
A studio when not in use.

DASH
DIGITAL AUDIO recorder using Stationary Heads.

DAT
DIGITAL AUDIO Tape.

DA VINCI
A DIGITALLY based preprogrammable colour corrector for film and videotaped pictures. It has a feature which allows selected areas of a picture to be colour corrected.

DAY FOR NIGHT
A procedure utilising underexposure and filters in the camera to give the impression of night time whilst shooting during the day.

DB
DECIBEL, one tenth of a Bel.

DBS
Direct Broadcasting from Satellite to individual dwellings without using master receiving stations or cable.

DCM
Dual Channel MONO.

DCS
Dual Channel STEREO.

DCT
Discrete Cosine Transform. The proprietary name of
the AMPEX Corporation for a family of acquisition and
post production DIGITAL COMPONENT Technology.

DEAF AID
An earphone used by presenters to receive instruction
from the GALLERY.

DECIBEL
One tenth of a bel, a logarithmic measure of power or
voltage, generally used to indicate AUDIO signal levels.

DECK
A videotape recorder/player in a post production edit
suite.

DECODER
A device which separates a COMPOSITE video signal
into its Red Green and Blue primary signals.

DEDIREC
A recording of a camera output by a specifically
assigned VTR.

DEGAUSSER
A device used for the rapid erasing of audio and
videotapes by passing the reels or CASSETTES
through a strong, magnetic field which is steadily
reduced to zero.

DEL
Direct exchange line. A temporary, dedicated
telephone communication circuit between an OB and a
studio centre.

DEPTH OF FIELD (OR FOCUS).
The distance between the nearest and furthest points
from a camera lens which are in acceptable focus after
the focus has been set.

DE - RIG
The dismantling of a studio or OB SET UP, including
the technical equipment.

DFS
DIGITAL FRAME STORE. A device which records TV
pictures as a DIGITAL signal for retention in computer
memory or HARD DISK for later recall.

DI BOX
Direct Injection box. A device which allows the
interfacing of electrical music instruments into a sound
mixing desk.

DIGIGRADE
The proprietary name of a DIGITAL film colour grading
system for use on a TELECINE machine.

DIGISCAN
A TELECINE machine that produces a TV image
composed of two INTERLACED FIELDS from the one
non-INTERLACED RASTER by using a DIGITAL image
store and reading out alternate TV lines.

DIGITAL
Referring to digits or computer numbers.
Much TV equipment now converts TV images into
digits so that they can be manipulated in a computer
and the results converted back into modified TV
images.

DIGITAL DUSTBIN
See A60-A66.

DIN
Deutsche Industrie Norm. The German standards
institute, commonly used to describe a type of multiway
AUDIO connector.

DIP
To reduce the sound level of one source in a sound mix
for a short period.

DIRECTOR
The person immediately charged with translating a
script into a TV programme, responsible for the artistic
interpretation and presentation.

DIRT
1. Director's Instant Reverse Talkback.
2. Direct Injected Reverse Talkback.
3. Director's Interrupted Reverse Talkback.
Three acronyms which refer to the same type of
system. viz. a talkback or intercom system, where one
Director can talk simultaneously to several Directors
and each of the recipients can respond by interrupting
the system to talk to the principal Director, a self muting
loudspeaker- type telephone sometimes being used.

DIRTY NETWORK FEED
A NETWORK feed of a TV broadcasters complete
transmission output.

DISC
A vinyl AUDIO record.

DISH
A saucer-shaped reflector used as part of a satellite or
microwave aerial system.

DISK
1. Diskette, an oxide coated flexible, mylar plastic disk
encased in a protective sleeve, also known as a floppy.
It is used to store DIGITAL data.
2. An oxide coated metallic platter used to store
DIGITAL data.

DISSOLVE
The gradual replacing of one video image by another
by reducing the signal of one image to zero whilst
simultaneously increasing the signal of the second
image from zero.

DLS
DIGITAL Library System. A device for storing still TV
images DIGITALLY on WINCHESTER DISCS under a
management system.

DMAC

Duobinary Multiplexed Analogue Components. A
television signal transmission ENCODING system
developed specifically for cable and satellite use. It has
the advantage over the PAL system of keeping the
LUMINANCE and CHROMINANCE COMPONENT
signals separate which prevents MOIRÉ and CROSS
COLOUR. It also provides the extra capacity to transmit
pictures in a 16:9 ASPECT RATIO which is better
suited for the televising of feature films. Multichannel
DIGITAL STEREO sound is also provided along with
additional data which can be used for payview
encryption.

D NOTICE

An official government announcement to news editors
to withold publication of material that the government
considers may prejudice national security.

DOC

Drop Out Compensator. A device built into most VTR
machines which replaces the missing TV lines of video
information with that of adjacent TV lines.

DOCKABLE

A CAMCORDER with an easily removable VTR.

DOCUDRAMA

A programme with a factual theme, shot in the method
of a DOCUMENTARY using dramatic performers.

DOCUMENTARY

A programme which presents historical, political and
social facts objectively, often using narration.

DOIL

Day Off In Lieu (of overtime payments).

DOLBY

The proprietary name of an audio tape NOISE
reduction system named after its inventor Ray Dolby.
Dolby A is a professional system,
Dolby B is a domestic system,
Dolby C is an enhanced domestic system,
Dolby SR is an enhanced professional system.

DOLLY
1. A wheeled camera mount. (N)
2. To move the camera. (V)

DOLPHIN ARM
The proprietary name of a short counterbalanced camera boom arm manufactured by VINTEN which can be used on various DOLLIES.

DOMESTIC CUT- OFF
That small fringe all round a TV picture which is not seen on a domestic TV receiver.

DOORSTEP
1. An unrehearsed interview with someone who is the subject of a news story, generally obtained by waiting outside the person's house.
2. To hound persistently someone who is newsworthy.

DOPE SHEET
A cameraman's list of shots and movements.

DOS
Disk Operating System. A collection of instructions and routines which allow a computer to operate. They are supplied on a FLOPPY DISK in the first instance.

DOT CRAWL
An ARTEFACT of the PAL colour TV system in which a pattern of moving dots appears in areas of saturated colours when displayed on a monochrome screen.

DOUBLE
A specialist performer who resembles and replaces a principal performer in scenes where an element of risk is involved. They are also used on LONG SHOTS as a cost effective measure.

DOUBLE HEADED
A film which has the sound recorded on a separate reel of sprocketed audio tape. The image and the sound start points are matched at the beginning (head) of the film and the film machine and audio follower electronically locked together to maintain synchronism.

DOWNSTAGE
A theatrical performing area nearest the camera or theatre audience.

DOWNSTREAM KEYER
A VIDEO KEYER which acts on the video output of a VISION MIXER.

DOWN THE LINE
To play out a programme, or part of it to another for preview or recording purposes prior to transmission.

DPA
DIGITAL Picture Archive. A high capacity library of TV images held on magnetic or optical discs in DIGITAL form.

DPC
DIGITAL Production Centre. A production centre from QUANTEL electronics consisting of a HARRY DIGITAL editing system, ENCORE HUD DVE, AND PAINTBOX.

DPE
DIGITAL Production Effects. A first generation DVE capable of limited 2 dimensional effects, manufactured by QUANTEL electronics. Generally known as the 'QUANTEL'.

DPS
1. Daily Planning Sheet. A document of work to be carried out against available resources.
2. Daily Programme Schedule. A chronological list of programmes to be transmitted. It contains the programme source, programme identification number, running time and other relevant details.

DRAMADOC
A dramatic reconstruction of a historic, social or political event using performers.

DRAPES
Hanging curtains or pieces of cloth which are used to decorate a SET.

DRESS
Preparation of a SET by the addition of PROPS,
cobwebs, smoke effects and the like.

DRESS REHEARSAL
A full rehearsal in costume and make up in a
DRESSED SET for the benefit of all concerned.

DRESS/TAPE
A system of recording studio sections of a programme
for subsequent editing by recording a TAKE of a
section immediately after its DRESS REHEARSAL.

DROP FRAME TIMECODE
An American version of TIMECODE in which two
FRAME counts are dropped every minute except the
tenth minute to allow for the difference between a
frame counter running at 30 fps (a sub multiple of
mains frequency) and the actual VIDEO FRAME rate of
29.97 fps.(as a result of a technical conflict between
colour and monochrome television systems.)

DROP-IN
A video image, or sound section INSERT EDITED into
existing material.

DROP-OUT
Visible image defects caused by the non recovery of
the signals from a section of videotape due to the loss
of magnetic oxide from the tape or poor head to tape
contact.

DROP-OUT COMP
A DROP-OUT compensator is a device built into most
VTRs that replaces the picture information missing due
to DROP-OUTS with that of adjacent TV lines.

DROP SHADOW
An electronic video effect consisting of a duplicated
silhouette of a character or image positioned behind it
and displaced both horizontally and vertically. It has
the effect of lifting the character or image from the
background picture, imparting depth to the composite
image and enhancing legibility against visually
conflicting backgrounds.

DRUM
The rotating assembly in a helical or transverse scan VTR which carries the VIDEO HEADS.

DRY (UP)
What happens when performers forget their lines.

DRY HIRE
The hiring of equipment without operational personnel.

DRY RUN
A studio rehearsal with performers but without technical crews.

DS
DOWNSTAGE, a script abbreviation.

DSIS
Dual channel Sound in Syncs — a method of conveying two AUDIO channels along with its associated VIDEO signal by converting the the audio to a DIGITAL signal and inserting it in the unseen video synchronising signal.

DSK
DOWNSTREAM KEYER.

DTF
Dynamic Track Following. The SONY developed method of ensuring the video head of a VTR passes over the recorded video tracks at varying linear tape speeds thereby providing broadcast quality images at variable speed.

DTS
Daily Transmission Schedule.

DUAL CHANNEL SOUND
A film or videotaped programme which contains two separate complete sound tracks, eg a programme with commentary in two languages.

DUB
1. To make a duplicate of the programme material of one tape from another.
2. To blend speech, music and effects on a film or videotape into one.

DUBBED
Generally made with reference to a foreign language film that has had the dialogue replaced with another language.

DUBBING EDITOR
The person who constructs the sound tracks prior to dubbing, using the CUTTING COPY as a guide.

DUBNER
An American manufacturer of broadcast hardware. Known specifically for its character generators.

DUCKER
An automatic sound DIPPER.

DUMP
1. A blank tape used to record material for immediate use and subsequently erased without creating all the tape storage documentation.
2. The process of transferring VIDEO images between DIGITAL HARDWARE by means of transmitting the digital data representing the pictures. It has the advantage of maintaining the picture quality and being much quicker than a video transfer.
3. The process of transferring computer data from a volatile electronic memory to a permanent medium such as a FLOPPY DISK.

DUP
Duplicate.

DUPE NEG
A duplicate negative made using a fine grain film.

DUPLEX
Simultaneous videotape recordings of the same source with identical TIMECODE.

DUTCH DOLLY
A three wheeled, rubber tyred, steerable camera mount generally used on OBs.

DVE
Digital Video Effects. A device that can manipulate and distort TV images into limitless forms by reorganising the DIGITAL data which represent the images.

DV(T)R
DIGITAL VIDEO (Tape) Recorder. A videotape recorder that records COMPONENT, COMPOSITE or DIGITAL TV images in the form of computer data. The main attribute of the system is the imperceptible GENERATION LOSS of the recordings.

DYNAMIC RANGE
The range of a signal, above the inherent noise level, that can be usefully handled by a device or system without imparting distortion.

EAGLE TOWER
A lorry mounted, 60ft. hydraulic tower with a remotely controlled panning head, used for the positioning of RADIO LINK transmitters and receivers which require line of sight for operation.

EBU
European Broadcasting Union, an association of European broadcasters for programming interchange and technical standards and recommendations.

EC
END CREDITS, a script abbreviation.

ECU
Extreme Close Up, a script abbreviation.

ECLAIR
French-made 16mm film camera used regularly on documentaries.

EDGE NUMBERS
Serial numbers and letters printed on the edge of unexposed negative film at each foot on 35mm film and every 6" on 16mm. They are used to enable negative cutters to match CUTTING COPY sequences (also known as key numbers).

EDGE TRACK
1. Sound recorded on the magnetic stripe alongside the images of a motion film.
2. Sound recorded along the edge of sprocketed magnetic tape.

EDIFLEX
A VIDEOCASSETTE based, OFF-LINE editing system which uses multiple VHS playback sources with TIMECODE to generate a U-MATIC MASTER and EDL for an ON-LINE editing system.

EDIT CONTROLLER
A computer based system which allows accurate control of the playback and record videotape recorders and associated peripheral equipment from TIMECODE numbers which are input from a keyboard.

EDITEC
The first commercial videotape editing system for QUADRUPLEX VTR machines developed by the AMPEX Corporation. It uses audio pips on the CUE TRACK to switch accurately between playback and record.

EDIT MASTER
1. A complete original edited videotape item or programme.
2. A full featured PC based edit controller capable of controlling up to six VTR machines.

EDITOR
The journalist charged with overall responsibility for the content of a news, or news magazine type, programme.

EDITOR (FILM)
The person who physically cuts the film and sound segments together and generally has some say in the shape of the finished programme.

EDITOR (VIDEOTAPE)
The person who operates the equipment that electronically edits videotape SECTIONS together and who generally has some say in the finished programme.

EDL
Edit Decision List. A list of VIDEO and AUDIO sources with associated TIMECODES and effects. Generated and used by a computerised videotape editing controller.

EECO
The Electronic Engineering Company, the American
company that developed TIMECODE.

E/E MASTER
An Electronically Edited (rather than physically cut)
master videotape. All videotape is now electronically
edited, but the convention remains.

E TO E
The video path through a VTR, from the input
electronics to the output electronics, (Entry To Exit)
bypassing the VIDEO HEAD.

EETPU
Electrical, Electronic, Television and Plumbing trade
union.

EFC
Electronic Film Conforming. The editing of film by
copying the film sections on to videotape with BITC to
provide an edited model as a guide for the NEG
CUTTER.

EFP
Electronic Field Production. The use of lightweight
VIDEO cameras and recorders on location, generally
for drama.

EFX
EFFECTS, a script abbreviation.

EGG CRATE
A device in the form of a rectangular grid of some depth
which when inserted into a studio lamp has the effect of
making the light beam parallel rather than divergent.
This produces almost 'shadowless' illumination.

EIDOPHOR
A BACK PROJECTION device in which a film of oil is
distorted by a VIDEO signal beam to produce an
image. The image is then illuminated by a powerful light
source and its reflection projected onto a screen
through a lens system.

ELAN
A videotape edit controller capable of controlling up to four VTRs, one recorder and three playback.

ELEMACK
The proprietary name of a film/video camera pedestal which runs on a rail track.

ELITE
A videotape edit controller capable of controlling three VTRs, one recorder and two playback.

ELS
EXTREME LONG SHOT, a script abbreviation.

EMBARGO
A programme which is prohibited from being screened for various legal or technical reasons.

E-MOTION
A computer programme that allows the HARRY digital editing system to control up to three VTRs from a displayed menu via its tablet and stylus.

EMMY
An award given by the Academy of Television Arts and Sciences of America for excellence of performance and production in the television medium. The name is derived from Immy which is slang for Image Orthicon, an early TV camera pick - up tube.

EMULSION
The light sensitive layer on the film base.

ENCODER
A device which combines the primary colour signals from an image generating device (eg TV camera or TELECINE etc.) together with the synchronising pulses to form a COMPOSITE VIDEO signal.

ENCORE
A two dimensional DVE manufactured by QUANTEL Electronics. It can be used as a component of a DPC and operated by means of a HUD.

END CREDITS
A list of participants and contributors which is run at the
end of a production.

END OUT
A film or videotape which has been projected or viewed
and is now on the take up reel. It must be rewound onto
the supply reel for further use.

END PROD
The identification or LOGO of a programme producing
company which appears at the end of their productions.

END SLATE
An inverted information board held in front of a camera
to signify the completion of a shot or the day's shooting.
It is also used to establish sound synchronisation when
this has not been established at the beginning of the
shot by operating the CLAPPER.

ENG
Electronic News Gathering. The use of VIDEO cameras
in place of 16mm film cameras for the acquisition of
news material.

EOP
End Of Part or End Of Programme.

EQ
Equalisation, the frequency selective amplification of a
signal to allow for selective losses in a system.

EQUITY
The actors' trade union.

ESD
A computerised videotape edit controller capable of
controlling up to six VTR machines, one recorder and
five playback.

ESS
Electronic Still Store. The proprietary name of a VIDEO
image store manufactured by the AMPEX Corporation
which records images on computer HARD DISKS.

ESTABLISHING SHOT
The foundation shot of a scene from which a finished sequence is woven through cutaways or reaction shots.

ETHERNET
A computer network system using COAXIAL cable as the data conductor, originally developed by Xerox.

EXEC PROD
Executive Producer. The person in overall charge of a production department or programme series.

EXCITER LAMP
A small bright lamp on a TELECINE machine which is used as the soundtrack analysing light source.

EXT
Exterior. A script abbreviation.

EXTRA
A person, not receiving individual direction, employed to be one of a crowd in a scene. *See* WALK ON.

EXTREME CLOSE UP
A camera shot revealing a small portion of a subject.

EXTREME LONG SHOT
A panoramic view.

EYELINE
The direction of an actor's look in relation to the camera.

F&E
Film & Equipment, generally refers to a type of screw - locking VIDEO cable connector originally used in the American film industry. Also known as PL-259 which is the US Signal Corps reference number.

FADE
The gradual reduction of a sound or vision signal to zero which results in the image and sound diminishing to black and silence respectively.

FAVOUR
To visually emphasise one subject of a group in a camera shot or direct a microphone to one of a group of performers.

FEEDBACK
A high pitched whistling noise in a sound system caused by a microphone picking up its own amplified output from a nearby loudspeaker.

FEMALE
A cable plug with sockets.

FERRIT
A magnetic tape sound player which can be synchronised to a TELECINE machine.

F/G
Foreground, a script abbreviation.

FIBRE OPTIC
A cable composed of thin fibres of glass which allows the transmission of a DIGITAL signal by means of light pulses.

FIELD
One field of a TV picture is the result of scanning the image by an electron spot from left to right and top to bottom (in the same manner as reading a page of print) and generating 312½ TV lines. Two fields interlaced together make one FRAME (or picture) of 625 lines in the TV system used in the UK and elsewhere.

FIELD DOMINANCE
The FIELD of a FRAME at which an edit occurs.

FIELD TAPES
VIDEOCASSETTE tapes which contain SECTIONS of unedited material from an outside (the studio centre) shoot.

FILL
1. A diffuse or soft light used to reduce the harshness and contrast of the KEY modelling light by lighting, (filling) the shadows.
2. To improvise by action or dialogue to conceal a technical shortcoming.

FILLER
Programme material used to fill a gap in the daily programme schedule. Sometimes known in advance or inserted on transmission by the PRESENTATION DIRECTOR.

FINAL MIX
The blending or dubbing of the music and effects tracks, with the commentary, to produce the final programme sound.

FINE CUT
Hopefully the final edit of a programme or film to fine tune or polish the previous edit. Sometimes necessary to make a programme fit an allocated time slot for transmission.

FISHEYE
A super wide angle camera lens used to impart dramatic distortion to an image.

FISHPOLE
A hand held telescopic microphone boom pole about 2 metres long used to assist in the positioning of a microphone.

FIT
Frame Interline Transfer. A type of CCD image transducer used in cameras in which the PIXEL information is read out on a line by line basis rather than being processed in a FRAME store and outputted after a processing delay thereby causing image smearing.

FLAG
A small GOBO which is used to shield light from a camera lens.

FLARE
1. Unwanted stray light entering a camera lens which reduces the contrast of the image.
2. A dazzling light caused by a highly reflective surface.

FLASH FRAME
1. An unintentional or unrelated FRAME of film or VIDEO in an edited sequence.
2. An overexposed frame of film caused by the film camera not having reached correct running speed from a start.

FLAT
A piece of background scenery constructed by stretching canvas over a wooded frame and painting it. *See* FLOAT

FLATBED
A film and soundtrack viewer and editor built on to a table.

FLEXIPOOL
Committees representing the ITV companies to decide the programming for transmission on the whole ITV NETWORK. Most companies proceed to the flexipool with PILOTS of proposed programme series, as expenditure on a whole series would be too risky prior to acceptance.

FLICKER STICK
A wooden stick with irregular strips of material attached along its length. When held in front of a studio LUMINAIRE and moved to and fro, it produces an effect similar to firelight.

FLIES
Hoists or wires suspended from the studio lighting GRID which are used to hoist (or fly) scenery upwards.

FLIP SIDE
The generally less commercial side of a single to the 'A' side.

FLOAT
A flat piece of scenery, normally on wheels, which can be easily moved for better camera access or to modify the foreground of a camera shot.

FLOATING POINT
A DIGITAL character generator with the ability to produce characters that appear to move in three dimensional space.

FLOPPY DISK
A form of computer data storage in the form of a thin OXIDE coated flexible plastic disc encased in a flexible sleeve.

FLOOR MANAGER
The person who is directly responsible to the studio DIRECTOR for the operation of the studio floor, cueing artists and studio discipline.

FLOOR PLAN
The layout drawing of the studio floor prepared by the programme designer. It is used by the scene crew to erect the scenery, the DIRECTOR to plan his camera shots, and by the LIGHTING DIRECTOR to assist in the lighting of the studio SETS.

FLUFF
An accidental dialogue error by an artist.

FLUTTER
Rapid variations in the speed of recording/playing
equipment.

FLY
1. To remove a curtain or piece of scenery by hoisting
upwards on fly wires.
2. To slide a foreground picture on or off screen,
revealing a background picture by means of a DVE.

FLY-BY
A VIDEO effect giving the illusion of a moving light
source by dynamically altering the position and size of
a DROP SHADOW.

FLYING ERASE
A VIDEO erase head which is mounted on the VIDEO
HEAD DRUM of a VTR to allow for the precise erasure
of individual VIDEO TRACKS. This is an essential
requirement for electronic editing purposes.

FLYING SPOT
A type of TELECINE machine where the film FRAME is
scanned by a flying spot of light from a CRT to produce
a VIDEO signal.

FM
1. FLOOR MANAGER.
2. Frequency Modulation - a modulation system where
the information to be carried varies the frequency of a
fixed frequency carrying signal.

FOC
Father Of the Chapel. The shop steward of an NUJ
branch.

FOLDBACK
A selected feed of sound from the studio mixing desk
fed to loudspeakers on the studio floor for the benefit of
performers.

FOLEY ARTIST
A person who matches their footstep sounds to filmed
images and operates various sound effect devices as
part of the sound post production process.

FOLLOW SPOT
A manned spotlight used to follow a performer during
their performance.

FONT
A set of typographical characters of the same style.

FOOT
The end of a reel of film.

FOOTPRINT
1. The area of the earth's surface served by a satellite
transmitting system.
2. Remnant encoding and decoding artefacts on a
VIDEO signal.

FORMAT
1. The process of preparing a blank FLOPPY DISK or
HARD DISK for use, by writing to all the tracks and
generating a directory (listing) of all free space. *See*
INITIALISE.
2. The layout of VIDEO and AUDIO tracks on a
videotape.

FOUNT
A set of typographical characters of the same style.

FOUR WALLER
A bare studio without any technical equipment installed,
the necessary equipment being hired separately by the
production company.

FOUR WIRE
A telephone communication system using separate
send and receive circuits.

FPS
FRAMES Per Second.

FRAME
1. A single image of a reel of film.
2. A single VIDEO image constructed by two
interleaved or INTERLACED FIELDS.

FRAMESTORE
A device used to hold TV FRAMES OR FIELDS in DIGITAL form on WINCHESTER DISKS, under a management system.

FREEZE
The repetition of one FRAME of film or VIDEO to produce a still picture in real time.

FRENCH BRACE
A strut used to support a FLAT, generally held in position on the studio floor by a STAGE WEIGHT.

FRENCH FLAG
A shield attached to a camera by a flexible rod to shade the camera lens from unwanted light.

FROM THE TOP
The rehearsal of programme material from the beginning of the programme or current scene which generally begins at the top of a page of the script.

FRONT AXIAL PROJECTION
A method of producing background scenic settings by projection from photographic transparencies or film at low intensity onto a highly reflective glass beaded surface so as not to affect the illumination of the foreground subject.

FRU
Fast Response Unit A small OB unit with on board RADIO LINK equipment for LIVE use at short notice.

FRYING
A hissing or crackling noise in sound equipment caused by a component failure or poor electrical connection.

FST
Flatter Squarer Tube. A new generation of CRT with improved geometry.

F/T
Film To Tape (transfer).

FTB
Fade To Black – a script abbreviation.

FULMAR
An extendible three tier camera pedestal.

FULLERS EARTH
A fine clay powder used by set designers.

F/X
Effects, electronic or practical.

FXLR
FEMALE XLR.

G SPOOL
A lightweight plastic videotape reel which can hold up
to 20 minutes of tape.

GAFFER
The senior lighting electrician of a film or VIDEO UNIT.

GAFFER TAPE
A canvas based heavy duty adhesive tape which is
used to secure anything to anything in a studio or
location.

GAMMA
The non linear relationship between the illumination of
a subject and the resulting density of film image or
amplitude of VIDEO signal.

GAMMA CORRECTION
The non linear predistortion added to a VIDEO signal to
ensure a linear change of illumination on a CRT face
for a linear change of signal at the input of a system.

GAMUT
In COMPONENT video, the 'gamut', or range of the
various signals must be controlled to avoid generating
illegal colour signals when converting into the red,
green and blue signals used by some equipment.
Some TV signal measuring equipment contains 'out of
gamut' indicators to warn of the generation of 'illegal'
colours.

GANTRY
The walkway around a studio lighting GRID.

GALLERY
1. A studio production control room.
2. An automated image library system by Rank Cintel.

GASH
Junk, generally refers to a short length of videotape left on a reel after the bulk has been removed. Used with great regularity in videotape editing suites to record short segments of material for immediate use.

GATE
The part of a film camera or TELECINE machine which holds the film in place behind the lens for the transmission of light through its aperture.

GEL
Jelly, a sheet of flame retardant coloured plastic positioned in front of a studio lamp to provide coloured illumination.

GENDER BENDER
An adapter for changing the sex of a cable plug.

GENERATION(LOSS)
The number of times that a recording is removed from the original LIVE action by subsequent DUBbing or re-recording. A recording of live action is the first generation, a recording of that recording is the second generation, and so on. Each generation perceptibly degrades the AUDIO and VIDEO image signals recovered from tape. Some VTR FORMATS degrade more than others. *See* D1, D2 etc.

GENLOCK
A system of electronically locking SPGs together such that the pictures based on the pulses from one SPG match the pictures based on the pulses from another SPG in time relationship. Hence picture signals generated from a remote location can be treated as a local source for vision mixing purposes.

GENNY
A mobile electric generator used to supply electric power to OB vehicles and equipment.

GFX
GRAPHICS, a script abbreviation.

GHOST
A faint horizontally displaced duplication of a TV image from a secondary signal resulting from reflections from obstacles such as buildings and aircraft etc.

GIGA
Prefix for one thousand million.

GLASS SHOT
A camera shot taken through a sheet of glass on which a part of a scene has been painted and which is then positioned in front of the camera lens to simulate actual scenery in a composite shot.

GLITCH
An undefined short term disturbance to an electrical system.

GNATS
A small movement of a camera, PROP or artist.

GOBO
An opaque material with irregular holes cut out, placed in front of a studio lamp to provide patterned illumination.

GOD SLOT
Term used to describe the hour between 1800 and 1900 on Sundays which is generally reserved for programming of a religious nature.

GOLDFISHING
Lip movements without accompanying sound.

GOOSE NECK
A microphone which is attached to the end of a flexible stalk for positioning near the user.

GPI
General Purpose Interface, a method of allowing systems to communicate with each other by means of electromagnetic relays.

GPN
GRAMPIAN

GRA
GRANADA

GRAB
The process of recording still VIDEO FRAMES from moving VIDEO images using a STILL STORE like a motorwind camera.

GRADING
1. The process of matching images on film sections due to differences in exposure, film stock and processing tolerances.
2. The process of electronically matching film images on a TELECINE machine by adjustment of the PRIMARY and SECONDARY colour VIDEO signals.
3. MONITORS — Grade 1 is a full broadcast reference colour balancing standard, Grade 2 is a general purpose standard, Grade 3 is a converted domestic TV receiver standard and is generally used for studio audience viewing.

GRAPHICS
Any visual material produced by a graphic artist.

GRAMPIAN
The ITV franchise holder serving the northeast region of Scotland.

GRANADA
The ITV franchise holder serving the northwest region of England.

GRAMS
A term used to describe the equipment in a studio sound control room that plays music or sounds into a studio, eg record deck, tape deck, CART player, CASSETTE player, CD player etc.

GRASS VALLEY GROUP
An American manufacturer of broadcast television hardware, especially renowned for its VISION MIXERS.

GREEN FILM
Film just received from the processing laboratory which has not completely dried out and can be easily damaged, the film EMULSION having a greenish appearance when not completely dry.

GREEN ROOM
The performers rest room in a theatre or TV studio. The name is derived from theatrical rest rooms whose decor tended to be green.

GREYSCALE
A camera test card that contains strips of accurately manufactured grey card ranging from black through increasing shades of grey to white. It is used for adjusting a colour TV camera to give faithful colour images.

GRID
A lattice of metalwork in the roof of a studio, from which studio lamps are suspended.

GRIP
A member of a film crew who is responsible for the movement of the camera.

GROUND ROW
A row of lamps placed on the studio floor (sometimes in a trough for concealment) which are used to light the CYC uniformly.

GUARANTEE ENGINEER
An engineer who accompanies a piece of equipment to ensure its correct performance.

GUARD BAND
The space left between individual VIDEO TRACKS on a videotape to prevent interference.

GUI
Graphical User Interface — a method of presenting computer programmes and tasks as ICONS on the screen. The programmes and tasks are initiated by moving a pointer on the screen to the icon and pressing a button on a keyboard or MOUSE.

GUIDE TRACK
A low quality reference sound track used for synchronisation purposes during POST PRODUCTION. It is replaced later by the full high quality soundtrack when available.

GUN MIKE
A specialised highly directional microphone. Used with good effect on DOCUMENTARIES and news gathering activities.

GV
General View. Material of a general nature, mostly panoramic views, which are used to establish a location.

GVG
GRASS VALLEY GROUP

GYROZOOM
A zoom lens with an inbuilt gyroscopic image stabiliser to minimise image blur caused by vibrations when shooting from a helicopter.

H/A
HIGH ANGLE, a script abbreviation.

HACK
A journalist.

HAD
Hole Accumulation Diode, a type of photoelectric
SEMICONDUCTOR diode used in the fabrication of TV
camera image sensors.

HAIRY
Troublesome or awkward in production.

HAND BASHER
Small hand held lamp. Generally used to illuminate
small areas or individuals whilst filming.

HAND HELD
A portable TV camera (N). Shot using same (V).

HARD COPY
The printed output from a computer which can be read,
rather than that which is electronically stored.

HARD LIGHT
Light from a LUMINAIRE which produces a well defined
shadow.

HARDWARE
The physical equipment and components of an
electronic system which, when related to computer
systems, require the addition of a list of instructions
(SOFTWARE) for the system to function.

HARLEQUIN
The proprietary name of an electronic picture colour corrector for the GRADING of VIDEO pictures produced from TELECINE or VTR. It has the ability to store up to 256 separate gradings which can be logged against TIMECODE for later recall.

HARRY
A random access DIGITAL VIDEO editing system which accepts VIDEO images in COMPOSITE, COMPONENT and DIGITAL formats which are converted into computer data for storage on WINCHESTER DISK drives. The disks can store up to the equivalent of 3024 still video FRAMES which represents 2 minutes of programme material at normal video rate of 25 FPS.

The system has a user friendly interface in that the video images from the two players and the recorder appear as three vertical filmstrips on a VIDEO picture monitor, the editing function being executed by an electronic stylus and tablet in conjunction with MENUS on the video picture monitor.

As the images are processed in the form of computer data, no degradation of the image quality occurs, and consequently the images can be re-recorded over and over again with additional material to build up multi-layered effects with no impairment to the original image. Due to the limited programme time capacity of the Winchester disks, each time a short sequence has been edited it is usually recorded on a DVTR thereby retaining the image quality and releasing the DISK storage of the system for the next piece of work.

HARRYTRACK
The AES/EBU DIGITAL STEREO soundtrack which follows the images edited on HARRY unless intentionally separated.

HARRIET
A DIGITAL graphics workstation with a dedicated FRAME STORE and VIDEO effects package.

HARRY SOUND
An interactive random access DIGITAL AUDIO editing
system which uses many of the concepts found in the
HARRY DIGITAL VIDEO editing system.
Consequently, when coupled together, they form the
basis of a fast post production workstation.
 The audio to be edited is presented to the user as a
visual display of reels of audio tape on a video monitor
with a menu of actions which are executed by using a
stylus and tablet as with the HARRY VIDEO editor.

HARRY SUITE
See DPC

HBO
Home Box Office, an American cable TV NETWORK
whose programming consists mainly of feature films.

HDTV
High Definition Television. A proposed new television
standard of 1250 lines and 16x9 ASPECT RATIO.

HEAD
1. The beginning of a reel of film or videotape.
2. The mechanical device used to mount a camera on
a tripod which allows camera movement in the
horizontal and vertical planes.
3. The electromagnetic transducer in a tape recording
system.

HEAD BANDING
An image defect on a QUAD VTR which is seen as a
series of horizontal bars of different brightness or
SATURATION due to maladjustment of the four VIDEO
channels.

HEAD CLOG
Full or partial loss of the sound or image from an
AUDIO or videotape recorder due to poor contact
between the magnetic pick-up head and the tape due to
tape OXIDE and/or other debris adhering to the head.

HEAD DRUM
A rotating metal drum which carries the VIDEO HEADS
in a HELICAL scanning videotape recorder.

HEAD LAMP
A camera mounted light for local supplementary illumination.

HEAD ROOM
1. The space between the top of SAFE PICTURE AREA of a TV image and the top of the subject's head.
2. The difference between the working level of an audio or video signal and the equipment design limits before distortion of the signal occurs.

HEAD OUT
A film wound on a reel where the beginning of the material leaves the reel first, ie ready for use.

HEAD SET
A combination of headphones and microphone used by camera and BOOM operators for dialogue with the production personnel in the GALLERY.

HELICAL(SCAN)
The manner in which videotape is wound around the rotating video HEAD DRUM in a VTR to achieve the necessary video track length to record one TV FIELD.

HELITRACK
An automatic microwave radio link tracking system for a helicopter borne MICROWAVE transmitter and TV camera.

HERON
A type of wheeled, hydraulic camera crane where control of the jib's elevation and camera platform rotation are controlled by the camera operator's foot pedals.

HERTZ
A unit of frequency (after Gustav Hertz). One Hertz equals 1 cycle per second.

HI-8
A videocassette FORMAT using metal particle tape 8mm wide developed by SONY for use in CAMCORDERS.

HIG
Hair In the Gate, a term used to indicate that debris, sometimes in the form of film shavings has appeared on the film image being viewed.

HIGH ANGLE
A camera shot taken from a high viewpoint relative to the action.

HIGH BAND
A video recording system which uses a higher carrier frequency in the modulation system to provide enhanced picture quality over the system it replaced, which is known as LOW BAND. Generally used with reference to 3/4" U-MATIC type VIDEOCASSETTE machines used for ENG.

HIGH HAT
A low camera mount which is used instead of a tripod.

HIGH KEY
Subject lighting where the tones generated are predominately at the light end of the brightness scale.

HMI
Halogen Metal Iodide. A gas discharge metal halide studio lamp of high light output and COLOUR TEMPERATURE similar to daylight.

HOLD
A static picture, generally a CAPTION, at the end of a programme or part of a programme to enable a smooth transition from one picture or programme source to another.

HOOK
A headline or other device which is used to persuade a viewer to continue watching, ie a trivial question at the start of a COMMERCIAL break with the answer coming at the end of the commercials.

HOP
1. A sudden sideways movement of a VIDEO image due to signal timing errors.
2. A sudden vertical bounce of a film picture due to mechanically poor film edits.

HORIZONTAL SYNC
Timing pulses that occur at the beginning of each line of a TV picture and are used to keep the scanning of the image generating device in step with the display device thus ensuring the image is correctly reconstructed.

HOSEPIPING
Excessive and erratic PANNING, TILTING and ZOOMING of a camera.

HOT
1. An excessively bright area on a studio floor in relation to surrounding areas.
2. Electrically live.

HOT FRAME
An overexposed film frame which is caused by the camera not running at the correct speed either during run up or run down. It is sometimes used as a cue mark.

HOT HEAD
The proprietary name of a remotely controlled pan and tilt camera mounting head.

HOT SEAT
A term used to describe the changing of production personnel during a COMMERCIAL break in a long running LIVE programme, eg 24 hour news programme.

HOT SPOT
An area on the studio floor of excessive illumination in comparison to adjacent light levels.

HOUSE LIGHTS
Lighting that is used whilst a studio is being prepared for use.

HOWL ROUND

A whistling or hooting sound in an AUDIO system caused by a microphone picking up its own amplified signal from a loudspeaker situated nearby. Known in certain quarters as "docking the ship".

H SHIFT

A video image disturbance where the complete image moves horizontally a small but perceptible amount due to a disruption of the PAL colour SYNCHRONISING signal.

HTV

The ITV broadcaster serving Wales and west England.

HUD

Head Up Display. A MENU driven interface for the QUANTEL ENCORE DIGITAL EFFECTS, using the same artist's tablet and electronic pen as the HARRY, HARRIET AND PAINTBOX systems.

HUE

One of the two attributes of a colour, the other being SATURATION.

HUM

Unwanted low frequency noise, typically around 50Hz, induced from surrounding mains powered circuits and equipment.

HUM BAR

Black horizontal bands running up or down a TV image due to some malfunction.

HYMN SHEET

A programme running order.

HYPER HAD

A HAD image sensor which has micro lenses fabricated over each diode for improved sensitivity.

Hz
Hertz, 1 cycle per second. A measurement of frequency of a periodic waveform, named after the German physicist Gustav Hertz.

IBA
The Independent Broadcasting Authority, the regulatory body for the ITCA and ILR now replaced by the ITC.

IBC
International Broadcasting Convention, a sales forum for broadcasting equipment.

IBM
International Business Machines, known as Big Blue due to its size and the colour of its LOGO. A multinational computer manufacturer with headquarters in the USA.

ICON
A graphic symbol identifier representing a function or process in a computer based system.

IDC
Insulation Displacement Connector. A wire connector that does not require the removal of the plastic insulation from the wire to make a connection. A connection is effected by displacing or cutting into the insulation by means of a sharp 'V' shaped metal contact in the connector.

IDIOT BOARD
A large cardboard sheet held near the camera with an artist's lines or prompts, to help avoid embarrassment.

ILLEGAL COLOURS
COMPONENT colour video signals which when ENCODED into the PAL COMPOSITE TV system produce signals outside its design limits.

IMAGE INTENSIFIER
A device which allows TV cameras to operate under
extremely low light levels.

IMAGE ORTHICON
An early type of camera pick-up tube in which the
image is focused on to a target which is orthogonally
scanned by an electron beam to convert the image into
a VIDEO signal.

IMAX
A wide screen motion picture system utilising high
quality images from 70mm film projected on to a screen
52 feet high and 64 feet wide. The auditorium is
specially constructed such that the screen occupies the
entire field of view of the audience thereby adding to
the sense of realism.

INDY
An independent producer of television progammes
without a licence to broadcast.

INFINITY CYC
A CYC brightly lit from GROUND ROWS in troughs
combined with a lit floor painted the same colour which
produces the effect of an infinite horizon.

INITIALISE
1. A power up sequence that puts a system in a
pre-operational state.
2. The preparation of a WINCHESTER DISK to receive
data. Generally only carried out once as any data
already resident on the disk is to all intents and
purposes lost, as the directory for the data is erased.
The data remains on the disk until it is overwritten by
new data. The 'lost' data can in most cases be
recovered by an expert using specialised information
and techniques.

INJECT
A LIVE programme segment from a remote source, eg
a news report.

INKIE-DINKIE
A very small, incandescent low powered light source.

INLAY
A VIDEO effect where parts of one image are laid into another.

INS
INSERT, a script abbreviation.

INSERT
A complete item recorded on videotape for playing into a studio programme.

INSERT EDIT
In video editing, an INSERT EDIT is one in which new images and/or sound are inserted into material already on the tape whilst leaving the CONTROL TRACK and TIMECODE unaltered. For operational ease, the preferred method of editing is to insert edit into a tape containing pre-recorded COLOUR BLACK, CONTROL TRACK AND TIMECODE. This prevents accidental over-recording of the control track by inadvertently being in assemble mode whilst attempting an insert edit. The disruption to the control track at the end of the assemble edit would render the tape unplayable.

INTEGRATED CIRCUIT
A collection of interconnected electronic components fabricated on a single crystal of silicon or other semiconducting material and generally encased in black plastic for protection.

INTERCUT
To CUT rapidly between two shots.

INTERNATIONAL M&E
An M&E soundtrack with continuous effects such that foreign speech can be over-DUBbed.

INTERNEG
A fine grain, low contrast duplicate negative copy of a master REVERSAL.

INTERPOS
A high quality fine grain, low contrast positive copy of a master negative film from which further negatives can be produced.

INTERVISION
The eastern European equivalent of the EBU.

IN THE CAN
A term used to signify that filming or recording has been completed.

INVISIBLE EDIT
A technically perfect COLOUR FRAMED VIDEO pick-up edit where there is no change of video source or parameters either side of the edit point.

INT
Interior, a script abbreviation.

IPPA
Independent Programme Producers Association.

IPS
Inches Per Second, linear tape speed.

IRIS
The variable opening in a lens system which regulates the transmission of light through it.

IRIS WIPE
A circular wipe effect.

IRN
Independent Radio News

ISLAND SITE
A regional TV centre which produces some local programming as well as programmes for its NETWORK.

ISO(FEED)
ISOlated feed. A term used to describe a camera whose output is fed exclusively to a VTR as well as being one of a group selected on a VISION MIXER for onward routing. Particularly useful in editing to widen the choice available to the DIRECTOR.

ITA
The International Television Association.

ITCA
The Independent Television Companies Association.

ITFC
Independent Television Facilities Company.

ITC
Independent Television Commission, the regulator of the ITV companies.

ITN
Independent Television News. The company funded by the ITV NETWORK and CHANNEL FOUR to provide them with a national and international news service. It also provides a service to the IRN and ORACLE.

ITS
Insertion Test Signals. A group of VIDEO test signals inserted at the top of FRAME, outside the picture area to test the quality of the transmission path.

ITV
Independent Television.

IV
In Vision, a script abbreviation.

IVCA
International Visual Communication Association. An association of corporate and non-broadcast programme makers formed by the merger of the British Industrial and Scientific Film Association (BISFA) and the International Television Association (ITA).

JACKFIELD
Rows of sockets for JACKPLUGS which allow access
to the inputs and outputs of AUDIO equipment in a
facility for the purpose of cross connecting or bypassing
equipment using PATCH CORDS.

JACKPLUG
A single pronged multisection plug for use in a
JACKFIELD.

JAMSYNC
The ability of a TIMECODE generator to lock its timing
circuits to an input of TIMECODE numbers from a
playback videotape such that the newly recorded
timecode increments sequentially from the previous
timecode.

JELLY
Slang for 'gelatine'. A sheet of coloured plastic film
placed in front of a LUMINAIRE to provide coloured
illumination.

JENNY
A mobile power generator.

JIMMY JIB
A portable camera boom which allows remote control of
the camera functions by the boom operator.

JINGLE
1. A short, catchy, repetitive piece of music used in
COMMERCIALS to help reinforce the product being
advertised.
2. An audible punctuation device in a radio programme
which is used as a STATION IDENT or introduction to a
road traffic or weather report.

JITTER
Small irregular movements of a picture.

JOG
Forward or reverse motion of film or videotape a FRAME at a time.

JOYBALLS
Recessed control balls in a console desk which allow continuous and relative adjustment of two parameters in a system.

JOYSTICK
A control lever in a console desk which allows relative adjustment of two parameters in a system.

JUKEBOX
A high capacity DPA.

JUMP CUT
An edit which disrupts the time continuity of a scene and shows artists or objects instantaneously changing place.

JUMPER
1. A short length of cable cable which is used to bypass or connect a circuit.
2. A JUMPSCAN TELECINE.

JUMPSCAN
A type of TELECINE machine where the film is scanned by the light from a CRT RASTER comprising two FIELDS positioned sequentially on the CRT face in the direction of film motion. The film FRAME is scanned by field one, and as the film traverses the CRT face it is then scanned by field two. To allow for the film movement across the tube face, the raster has to 'jump' across the tube face back again every 1/25th of a second.

JUNCTION
The period between two programmes which is usually filled by commercial advertising, on-air promotions, announcements or station identification.

JVC

JVC
The Victor Company of Japan, the developer of the VHS domestic VIDEOCASSETTE recorder.

K

K
1. KILO.
2. KELVIN.

K FACTOR
A measure of the response of a circuit handling
repetitive waveforms (eg VIDEO signals) using a
special test signal and OSCILLOSCOPE graticule.

K SPOOL
A lightweight plastic videotape reel containing up to
nine minutes of tape. Generally used for the physical
transportation of COMMERCIALS or short programme
material.

KADENZA
A DIGITAL picture processor from GRASS VALLEY.

KALEIDOSCOPE
A DVE from GRASS VALLEY.

KELVIN
Temperature measurement on the Kelvin scale. Used
as an indicator of the colour of a light source, eg a
studio lamp which indicates 2750° K on a colour
temperature meter would produce warm or reddish skin
tones compared to a lamp measuring say 3200° K
which would produce cold or bluish skin tones.

KERNING
The process of adjusting the horizontal positioning of
typographical characters to enhance clarity and
presentation. (The KERN is that portion of a character
which projects beyond the body or shank of the
character.)

KESTREL
The proprietary name of a wheeled camera mount manufactured by VINTEN, which consists of a platform with a seat and camera mount, on the end of a boom arm which can be raised from 2 to 7ft above ground level.

KEY
1. Key light, the main modelling light for the centre of interest in a scene.
2. A VIDEO effect where parts of one image are cut into another, the area of replacement being determined either by the LUMINANCE or CHROMINANCE values of the first image.

KEYCODE
Machine readable KEY NUMBERS. The film equivalent of TIMECODE developed by Kodak.

KEY GRIP
The senior GRIP on a film UNIT.

KEY NUMBERS
See EDGE NUMBERS.

KEYSTONE DISTORTION
A geometric distortion to an image which results in converging verticals.

KHz
One thousand HERTZ.

KICKER
A small supplementary light used to illuminate a small area of a subject to enhance modelling.

KILL
Switch off (eg a studio LUMINAIRE). Stop.

KILO
Prefix for one thousand.

KILOWATT
One thousand watts, a measure of electric power consumed by studio lamps. Used as an indication of their strength of illumination.

KOPERNICUS
A DBS satellite.

KU BAND
The super high frequency band around 11GHz set aside for DBS.

KURL
An enhancement to the KALEIDOSCOPE which produces curved distortions to video images.

KW
Kilowatt.

L

L/A
LOW ANGLE, a script abbreviation.

L CUT
An edit in which the video and audio edits occur at different positions on the tape.

LACE UP
To thread film through a TELECINE machine or projector for projection.

LAG
The remnant, but fading image of a bright, moving, televised subject due to the inability of the camera pick-up tube to react instantly to such changes.

LANDLINE
The BT countrywide NETWORK of VIDEO and AUDIO cable circuits.

LAVALIER
A small microphone hung around the neck, pendant fashion.

LAYBACK
Recording the final mixed sound back on to the edited master videotape.

LAYOFF
To playback the audio from an edited master videotape to a SOUND DUBBING suite for SWEETENING or SOUND POST PRODUCTION.

LAZY TALKBACK
A talkback or intercom system which uses a
commentator's or presenter's microphone for
production
talkback as well as the programme sound. The purpose
of the microphone is selected by use of a nearby
switch.

LE
Light Entertainment.

LEADER
1. The film at the beginning of a reel, used for
identification, cueing, lacing and protection purposes.
2. The coloured plastic tape attached to each end of an
AUDIO tape for threading and protection purposes.

LED
Light Emitting Diode. A solid state semiconductor
which emits light on application of a voltage.

LEDDICON
The proprietary name of a type of lead oxide camera
pick up tube.

LEGS
A camera tripod.

LENS CAP
A protective metal or plastic disc which fits over the
lens when not in use.

LENS HOOD
A shield fitted to a lens to prevent unwanted light
entering the lens and causing FLARE.

LETTERBOX
A method of transmitting a WIDE SCREEN film on a
TV screen of 4x3 aspect ratio, by utilising the full width
of the film image on the TV screen with the consequent
reduction in height of the image.

LIFT
To record the sound tracks from a film for dubbing and
mixing purposes.

LIGHTING CAMERAMAN
A senior film cameraman who is responsible not only for the pictorial composition but also the lighting of a scene.

LIGHTING DIRECTOR
The person responsible for the creative lighting of a production.

LIGHTING GRID
A matrix of girders in a studio ceiling from which LUMINAIRES are hung.

LIGHTING RIG
A group of LUMINAIRES and associated equipment required to illuminate a scene.

LIMES
Limelight, an early type of large follow spotlight whose illumination was produced by incandescing calcium oxide (lime).

LINE
1. One of the 625 horizontal scanning lines in a TV camera which analyse a scene to produce a TV image in the UK TV system.
2. A short piece of scripted dialogue.

LINE BLANKING
The period in between success TV lines during which the VIDEO signal is blanked out to allow for the invisible retrace of the scanning spot.

LINES
1. The technical area of a facility where incoming and outgoing vision and sound circuits are connected to their destinations after being technically assessed.
2. A performers scripted dialogue.

LINES BOOKINGS
The office of a facility concerned with the booking of incoming and outgoing vision and sound circuits on a TV NETWORK.

LINE SWITCH
The automatic rerouting of the television and sound circuits carried out at NSCs by BRITISH TELECOM to a prearranged schedule between the broadcasters and BT.

LINE SYNC
A pulse which occurs at the start of every TV line which ensures synchronisation of the scanning process in a TV system.

LINE UP
Preparation time prior to transmission or recording, for adjusting all the equipment involved for optimum performance and verifying vision and sound circuits.

LINKS
A method of relaying the vision and sound from a remote OB location by means of super high frequency radio transmissions to a suitable receiving point, for use in a central technical area for transmission or recording.

LIP FLAP
Lip movements without accompanying sound.

LIP MIKE
A specialised screened microphone which is held close to the mouth to reduce the pick-up of unwanted nearby sounds.

LIP SYNC
The exact synchronisation of image with soundtrack, most noticeable when performers speak their LINES.

LIQUID GATE
A device used in a film printer or TELECINE machine in which a liquid of the same refractive index as the film base is flushed over the surface of the film to 'fill in' scratches and remove debris.

LIVE
Transmitted as it occurs.

LMS (Library Management System.)
The proprietary name of a highly automated, high
capacity multi-CASSETTE VTR system manufactured
by the SONY CORPORATION, which requires only the
input of a playlist to sustain its output of programmes
and COMMERCIALS from up to six VTR CASSETTE
players / recorders.

LOCAL END
Vision and sound circuits from a facility to the nearest
NSC.

LOCKED
A term used to signify that a videotape recorder has run
up to the correct operating speed and is now recording
recoverable pictures.

LOF
Left Of (PICTURE) Frame, a script abbreviation.

LOGO
An identifying symbol or trade mark.

LOGOMASTER
An addition to the ASTON 4 and Aston CAPTION
character generators which produces multicoloured
LOGOS from original artwork and a monochrome video
camera.

LOG-ON
1. The process of acquiring exclusive access to a
CAPTION generator which supports more than one
typewriter style keyboard.
2. The process of gaining access to to a computer
NETWORK, generally requiring the use of a password
to identify the user.

LONDON WEEKEND TELEVISION
The ITV broadcaster serving the London area from
Friday evening to Monday morning.

LONG SHOT
With reference to a person, a head to toe-ish camera
shot.

LOOP
1. An endless piece of film used for test and alignment purposes.
2. An endless piece of AUDIO tape for producing a continuous sound effect.

LOOPING
The post production process of adding dialogue to a film section by artists viewing a continuous LOOP of film which shows the same scene repeatedly. This allows artists several attempts at matching their voice to their filmed lip movements.

LOT
The area of ground within a companies' premises that can be used for the construction and erection of exterior SETS.

LOW ANGLE
A camera shot taken from below the the main action or the performer's eyeline.

LOW BAND
A U–MATIC type VIDEOCASSETTE recorder used for archival and viewing purposes. The machine does not record pictures of broadcast quality.

LOW KEY
A picture whose light values are predominately at the dark end of the scale.

LOUMA
The proprietary name of a long boom arm type of camera mount with a lightweight remotely controlled camera attached, for obtaining otherwise inaccessable camera views. *See* HOT HEAD.

LRU
Location Recording Unit. A two camera OB mobile control room, with one camera having the ability to be used in the 'CAMCORDER' mode.

L/S
1. LONG SHOT, a script abbreviation.
2. Loudspeaker.

LTC
Longitudinal TimeCode. A DIGITAL signal recorded along the length of an AUDIO or VIDEO tape to identify individual image FRAMES. The signal is used by various equipment as a means of locating material on the tape, eg computerised edit controllers.

LUMEN
The unit of luminous flux, a measurement of the quantity of light from a source of one CANDELA.

LUMINAIRE
A generic name given to studio lamps.

LUMINANCE
The electrical signal that relates to the brightness of a TV picture.

LUMINANCE KEY
A VISION MIXER VIDEO effect in which areas of a foreground picture which exceed a preset brightness level, are cut into a background picture.

LWT
LONDON WEEKEND TELEVISION.

LUX
The unit of illumination, equal to one LUMEN per square metre.

MII(M2)
A 1/2" COMPONENT ANALOGUE VIDEOCASSETTE
system developed by Panasonic to compete with the
BETACAM system from Sony.

M&E
Music and Effects, a POST PRODUCTION DUB
containing only music and background ambient sounds.

M&S
Main & Side, the two components of a STEREO
AUDIO signal where MONO compatibility is required,
the Main comprising of the left plus right channels (the
MONO signal) and the Side comprising of the left
minus the right channels (the STEREO information).

MAC
1. Macintosh, a family of personal computers
developed by the APPLE corporation which boast a
unique GUI.
2. Multiplex Analogue Component signals, a
transmission system developed by the IBA for
television broadcasting from satellite.

MACRO
A sequence of computer keystrokes that can be stored
and accessed by a single user-defined key.

MAGENTA
The complementary colour to green in the TV spectrum
produced by mixing red and blue.

MAGIC ARMS
A rod assembly with two or three ball and socket joints
which is used to position a FRENCH FLAG by a
camera or LUMINAIRE.

MARC
M II(2) Automated Recording and playback Cassette system.

MAIN(FEED)
The videotape recorder that records the output of a studio or OB VISION MIXER.

MALE
A cable plug with pins.

MARCO POLO
A high power extraterrestrial communications satellite for DBS use.

MARK IT!
An instruction to a CLAPPER LOADER to operate the CLAPPER BOARD at the beginning or end of a TAKE.

MARK UP
To place visible indications on a film or videotape as an aid to locating the required material.

MARRIED PRINT
A POSITIVE film print containing both the visual image and the associated sound track.

MASTER
1. MCR
2. The first complete edited version of a videotaped programme.
3. A complete original film print from which DUPE NEGS are made.

MASTER SHOT
A wide angle establishing shot.

MASTER/SLAVE
A system of recording VIDEO material on two VTR machines, one of which (the master) records the mixed source output and the other (the slave) records specific sources. Both VTR machines are fed with the same TIMECODE as a means of locating the required material during editing. *See* MAIN feed and ISO feed.

MATCH FRAME EDIT
A VIDEO edit which maintains the PAL four FRAME sequence of synchronising signals and therefore produces no horizontal or vertical picture shifts across the edit.

MATRIX WIPE
A VIDEO transition produced by a VISION MIXER, the boundary between the pictures being the combination of a pseudo-random pattern of small picture tiles along a preselected boundary shape.

MATTE
An electronic or optical opaque image mask.

MATTE FILL
A VIDEO KEY effect where the FILL is derived from a MATTE GENERATOR

MATTE GENERATOR
A component of a VISION MIXER that generates a uniform coloured VIDEO FRAME.

MATISSE
A graphics PAINTING system.

MCPS
Mechanical Copyright Protection Society.

MCR
1. Master Control Room, the area in a broadcasting facility where programmes, COMMERCIALS and on-air PROMOTIONS are linked together, sometimes with the aid of a station announcer, under the control of a PRESENTATION DIRECTOR in order to provide a continuous station output to the transmitter.
2. Mobile Control Room as used on OBs.

MCU
MEDIUM CLOSE UP, a script abbreviation.

MEDIA COMPOSER
A DIGITAL NON LINEAR VIDEO editing system which
stores the digitised video images on high capacity
WINCHESTER DISKS for rapid random access. The
images are not of broadcast quality but the EDL
produced from the model of the programme can be
input to an ON-LINE edit facility to produce broadcast
quality video recordings.

MEDIUM CLOSE UP
A breast-pocket level camera shot.

MEDIUM LONG SHOT
With reference to a person, head to knee level camera
shot.

MEGA
Prefix for one million.

MENU
1. A list of instructions on a computer display.
2. A chronological list of the items in a programme or
transmission sequence.

MER
MERIDIEN

MERIDIEN
The ITV franchise holder covering the south of
England.

MHz
MegaHertz, one million HERTZ per second.

MIC
Microphone.

MICRO
The prefix for one millionth.

MICROWAVE
Super High Frequency Radio waves above 1GHz which
are used for point to point transmission of VIDEO
signals.

MID SHOT
A waistline to top of head camera shot.

MIDI
Musical Instrument Digital Interface, an international specification for the connecting of musical instruments into DIGITAL equipment.

MILLI
The prefix for one thousandth.

MIPCOM
International film and programme market for TV, video, cable and satellite, held in Cannes, France.

MIP TV
An international TV programme sales forum held in Cannes, France.

MIRAGE
A three dimensional picture manipulator which transforms live action into three dimensional shapes that can change from one form to another in three dimensional space.

MIX
The adding of sound sources together at differing sound levels to produce the complete composite sound.
In VIDEO terms, a mix is the gradual dissolving of one picture into another.

MIXER
A device for the mixing, processing and routing of various AUDIO and VIDEO sources. *See* CLEAN FEED (SOUND)

MIX-MINUS
A programme sound MIX of all sources except that of the recipient of the feed.

MIZAR
A 300–500 watt compact focusing spotlight, used for concealed lighting.

MLS
MEDIUM LONG SHOT, a script abbreviation.

MODEM
MOdulator/DEModulator. A device that allows DIGITAL signals to be carried along ANALOGUE circuits.

MOLE
Mole Richardson, the proprietary name of a power driven wheeled camera mounting, in which the camera is mounted on a counterbalanced arm which can be manually raised and lowered.

MOIRÉ
Visible patterning on a video image due to inherent deficiencies in the signal system, causing the generation of unwanted signals.

MONITOR
1. A high quality video display screen for TV images derived from a video signal rather than from a broadcast transmitter.
2. A high quality loudspeaker for assessing sound in a control room or production gallery.

MONOCHROME
Generally used to refer to a black and white image.

MONTAGE
A composite group of either dynamic or static thematic camera shots or images.

MOONSHOT
The proprietary name of a lorry mounted hydraulic platform capable of being raised to a height of 46 metres.

MORPHING
The smooth transformation of one VIDEO image into another by computer manipulation of the digital data representing the image.

MOS
Mit Out Sprechen! (an American corruption of the German). Silent filming of a subject.

MOSAICING
A DVE effect in which a TV image is broken into tiles of uniform size, colour and brightness. The tile size can be varied from one PIXEL which is the same as having no mosaicing, to a significant portion of the full picture.

MOUSE
An alternative to a typewriter keyboard as an input device for a computer system. It consists of a pod which can be moved over the desk surface, and whose movements affect the position of a pointer on the computer screen. The pointer is positioned over ICONS or MENUS of instructions on the screen and a button on the pod depressed to initiate the instruction.

MRS
1. Music Recording Studio.
2. Music Recording Session.

M/S
MID SHOT, a script abbreviation.

MU
The Musicians Union.

MULTILATERAL
A satellite TRANSPONDER which is timeshared by more than one communications company.

MULTITRACK
An audio tape recorder with more than four audio tracks.

MUSA
A push-on video connector used on patch panels for the temporary cross-connecting of VIDEO circuits.

MUSIC CIRCUIT
A special BT audio circuit capable of carrying signals of broadcast quality.

MUTE
Images without sound.

MVTR
Mobile Video Tape Recorder.

MXLR

MXLR
MALE XLR.

NAB
National Association of Broadcasters
An association of American radio and TV broadcasters
specifying standards and promoting the interests of the
broadcasting industry.

NAB CART
A standard audio tape CARTRIDGE of dimensions
specified by the NAB, some times called SPOT CART.

NAB SPOOL
A 26.6cm diameter audio tape reel of specification
defined by the NAB which has a large central hole for
locating on a tape deck hub.

NADGERS
1. A small movement of a camera or PROP.
2. Disturbance or jitter on a TV camera picture.

NAGRA
The proprietary name of a specialised portable reel to
reel tape recorder that contains synchronising circuits
which make it very useful as a film sound recorder.

NARRATION
Dialogue spoken over pictures.

NBC
National Broadcasting Corporation, one of the three
major American commercial TV networks.

NC
NewsCaster, a script abbreviation.

NCR
NETWORK Control Room, The technical area of a
broadcasting facility concerned with the routing of
programme material to and from a NETWORK.

NCIV
NewsCaster In Vision, a script abbreviation.

ND FILTER
Neutral Density Filter. An optical filter used to reduce
the amount of light reaching the image transducers in a
camera without reducing the lens aperture or affecting
the colour balance.

NDF TIME CODE
An American version of TIMECODE in which the
FRAME count is a continuous repetition of 30 frames
for every second of video material. For technical
reasons, the American TV video frame rate is actually
29.97 per second and it follows therefore that this form
of timecode is not synchronous with REAL TIME.

NECAM
NEve Computer Assisted Mixing desk.
A sound mixing desk manufactured by Neve
Electronics in which the channel fader positions and
various trigger signals can be stored on a computer for
later recall.

NEEDLE DROP
The authorised individual use of a copyrighted musical
piece by the purchase of a licence from the copyright
holder.

NEEDLE TIME
An agreement between the MU and radio broadcasters
concerning the ratio of recorded to live music used.

NEG
Negative film.

NET
NETWORK, a script abbreviation.

NETWORK
Several radio or TV stations linked together for the purpose of simultaneous transmission from a nominated programming source.

NEVE
Neve Electronics, a manufacturer of sound mixing desks.

NEWSTAR
A newsroom computer system used by journalists and technical staff in the preparation of a news programme.

NEWTONS RINGS
Light interference patterns in the form of coloured rings which appear at glass to glass or glass to film surfaces.

NG
No Good.

NHK
The Japanese state broadcasting authority.

NI-CAD
A portable, high capacity rechargeable battery containing NIckel and CADmium electrodes.

NICAM
Near Instantaneous Companded Audio Multiplexed, a DIGITAL STEREO sound transmission system for television developed by the BBC.

NIGGER
A shield positioned near a light or camera lens.

NIKE
The proprietary name of a battery driven, long boom arm type wheeled camera mounting manufactured by Chapman.

NITRATE FILM
An obsolete highly inflammable film base made from cellulose nitrate whichrequires careful handling as it is impossible to extinguish once alight.

NLE
NON LINEAR EDITING

NODDY
A camera shot of an interviewer nodding their head in an understanding manner for CUTAWAY editing into an interview.

NOISE
A random and persistent electrical disturbance generated within electronic equipment that affects the clarity and quality of a signal. The effect of noise on an AUDIO signal is to produce hiss, whilst the effect of noise on a VIDEO signal is to produce grain or snow on the picture.

NON-COMP
A VIDEO signal without any synchronising pulses.

NON LINEAR EDITING
An editing process that allows images to be assembled out of sequence as in film.
In the video domain the video images are DIGITISED and stored on high capacity WINCHESTER DISK drives which allow random access to the image data.

NORTH LIGHT
A large soft FILL light with a COLOUR TEMPERATURE similar to an overcast northern sky.

NOS
Nederlandse Omroep Stichting, the Dutch state broadcasting organisation which acts as regulator for commercial broadcasters.

NOTE
An instruction or small amendment to an artists performance from the director during rehearsal or before a TAKE.

NOTIONAL
A replacement midweek rest day for weekend workers.

NR
Norsk Rikskringkasting. The Norwegian state
broadcasting organisation

NSC
Network Switching Centre. Centralised locations in the
BT communications NETWORK which control and
monitor the switching of circuits between broadcasters
and transmitters.

NTL
National Transcommunications Limited. The company
responsible for the operation and maintenance of the
transmitter NETWORK for ITV.

NTSC
National Television Systems Committee, the body that
specified the American 525 line colour TV system and
whose name it bears.

NUMBER
A number, identifying the scene about to be shot which
appears on the SLATE or CLAPPER.

NUJ
The National Union of Journalists.

OB
OUTSIDE BROADCAST.

OCP
Operational Control Panel

OIRT
Orgination International Radio et Television, The East European association of broadcasters.

OFF-AIR
The reception of a programme via a broadcast transmitter.

OFF-LINE EDIT
The editing together of programme sections on low cost non broadcast equipment to provide a model to work from. Some off - line edit systems can produce an EDL for use in a broadcast quality ON-LINE edit suite.

OFF MIKE
A sound source that is outside the designed response area of a microphone and therefore does not generate the correct level of signal, sometimes used intentionally to imply distance.

OFF THE AIR
A technical breakdown situation where no programmes are transmitted.

OFF THE TUBE
A term used to describe the act of commentating on a live sports event by viewing the action on a VIDEO MONITOR screen rather than being present at the location.

ON-AIR
A programme being transmitted.

ONE LEGGED
A malfunction in a sound system where one wire of a screened pair cable is disconnected with a consequent reduction in signal level and increase in NOISE and HUM.

ONE LIGHT
A film print obtained by setting the printer light source to an acceptable average value.

ON THE BLINK
Faulty.

ON THE FLY
In video editing, the act of marking an edit point on a tape as it is being played.

ON-LINE EDIT
The editing together of sections of VIDEO material by a computer controlled editing system to produce a complete edited broadcast quality master videotape for playback or transmission.

OOS
Out Of Sync, the non synchronisation of sound with image.

OOV
Out Of Vision, a person who is heard but not seen.

OPEN MIKE
A microphone that is faded up on a sound desk.

OPEN TALKBACK
An inter-area communication system in which the principal can be received at all destinations that are assigned by latching the speak key open.

OPTICAL TRACK
Sound in the form of a narrow, variable width or variable density image alongside the film frames of a motion picture.

OPTICALS
Special visual effects on film that are generated by optical means, eg FADES, MIXES, WIPES etc.

ORACLE
The TELETEXT system developed by the IBA and used on the ITV NETWORK.

ORF
The Austrian state broadcasting organisation.

OS
Overnight SET.

OSCAR
An annual award in the form of a small golden statuette given by the Academy of Motion Picture Arts and Sciences to individuals in recognition of achievement in their art or craft. Named after the likeness of an official's uncle.

OSCILLOSCOPE
An electronic measuring instrument which produces a graph of an electrical signal on a CRT .

OSL
Overnight SET and Light.

OSS
Over Shoulder Shot, a camera shot taken over the shoulder of a person in the foreground.

OTT
Over The Top, excess. Normally applied to an over-enthusiastic performance by an artist.

OUTAGE
Programmes not being transmitted from a broadcast transmitter due to planned maintenance.

OUT OF SYNC
Non coincidence of image and sound.

OUTSIDE BROADCAST
A programme which takes place at a location outside or away from a broadcaster's studio centre.

OUTTAKE
A TAKE of a scene that does not appear in the final edit of a film or programme. *See* TRIMS.

OVERCRANK
A term used to signify a film camera running at more than normal speed with the result that any movement will be slowed down when the film is projected at normal speed.

OVERRECORD
To record over, and hence erase material already on tape that is not required.

OVERRUN
To exceed the planned filming or studio time.

OVERSCAN
To scan in excess of the target area of a camera pick-up tube to reveal the boundary of the image on a monitor. This is necessary to ensure central location of the image on the target when setting up a camera for use after tube replacement.

OXIDE
The coating material on AUDIO or VIDEOtape that is magnetised during the recording process.

P as B
Programme as Broadcast.
A document containing details of all the legal and financial responsibilities of the programme broadcaster.

P as C
Programme as Completed
A document containing details of all the legal and financial responsibilities of the programme production company.

P as R
Programme As Recorded
A document for the use in a presentation department containing details of the duration of the programme parts, when the closing CREDITS appear, etc. Information is either supplied by the PA of the programme or is ascertained by presentation staff previewing the programme prior to TX.

PA
1. Production Assistant, the programme DIRECTOR'S assistant and co-ordinator. Responsible for the administration and logistical support of the programme, and the DIRECTOR!
2. Press Association, an international news agency.
3. Public Address System.

PACK SHOT
1. Close up shot of an item or product in an advert.
2. A static shot of a PROP or props for reference or demonstration purposes.

PACT
The Producers Alliance for Cinema & Television.
Formed by the merger of the IPPA and TPA.

PAG BELT
A belt containing heavy duty rechargeable batteries for powering a film or video camera or hand held lights.

PAINTBOX
The proprietary name of a VIDEO graphic production device manufactured by QUANTEL Electronics that allows the results of an electronic pen and artist's tablet to be reproduced on a TV MONITOR. The system has a palette of colours and other attributes that can be accessed by the pen on a MENU appearing at the bottom of the TV monitor screen.

PAINTING
The act of electronically modifying a VIDEO image by means of a PAINTBOX or similar device.

PAINT POT
A JOYSTICK control on a VISION MIXER which allows the selection of any colour from the PAL palette to colour MONOCHROME CAPTIONS .

PAL
Phase Alternate by Line, the colour TV system used in the UK, most of Europe and elsewhere. A single image (FRAME) in this standard consists of two INTERLACED FIELDS of 312½ scanned lines of video information and 25 frames are produced every second.

PALTEX
A manufacturer of computerised videotape edit controllers.

PAN
To pivot a camera in a horizontal direction.

PANAGLIDE
A camera harness which allows smooth hand held operation of a motion picture camera.

PANAVISION
A WIDE SCREEN 35mm film process using an ANAMORPHIC lens to laterally compress the image. A complementary lens on the projector expands the image to the ASPECT RATIO of the original scene.

PANCAKE
A film wound on a CORE.

PANSCAN
The process of televising a film of an ASPECT RATIO other than the standard 4x3 ASPECT RATIO of the TV screen. The film FRAME is made to fill the TV screen height which results in parts of the image being lost from each edge. By electronically moving the scanning RASTER of the TELECINE machine horizontally across the film FRAME the main centre of action can be followed.

PAN STICK
Oil based foundation make-up in the form of thick crayon stick.

PATCH CORD
A short audio or video cable used on a PATCH PANEL.

PATCH PANEL
A panel on an equipment rack consisting of rows of audio or video sockets for the cross-connecting or bypassing of equipment using PATCH CORDS.

PAYOFF
A reporter's concluding remarks on an investigative story.

PB
PULL BACK, a script abbreviation.

PBS
Public Broadcasting Service. An American educational and entertainment network.

PBX
PAINTBOX.

PC
A Personal Computer (IBM type)

PCM
Pulse Code Modulation. A modulation system used to provide high quality AUDIO in some VTRs.

PC&OP
Protection Circuit and Occasional Programme. Back-up VISION and sound circuits in a television NETWORK that can be utilised for the exchange of material between contractors on the understanding that if the primary circuit fails, they will be commandeered without notice.

PEAK WHITE
The brightest image level or video signal level a TV system can handle.

PED
Pedestal
1. A wheeled studio camera mounting in which the camera can be raised or lowered with little effort due to the use of gas filled pistons.
2. The amount by which the signal parameter that specifies the black areas of a picture is above BLANKING LEVEL.

PENGUIN
The proprietary name of a track mounted camera DOLLY manufactured by Vinten, sometimes used with a DOLPHIN ARM.

PER DIEM
A daily food and accommodation allowance for location workers.

PERFECTONE
The proprietary name of an audio player for a TELECINE machine

PERFORATIONS
Rectangular holes along the edge(s) of film to allow for its movement and registration in the GATE.

PETER PEARCE
The proprietary name of a device which measures the relationship between SUBCARRIER and LINE SYNC pulse in a COMPOSITE video signal, a critical reference in the videotape editing environment.

PF
PRE FADE, a script abbreviation.

PFL (Piffle)
Pre-Fade(r) Listen, the ability to listen to a sound source on a sound mixing desk before it is faded up.

PGM
1. Programme.
2. The main output of a VISION MIXER.

PHANTOM
A process whereby the power supply for a microphone is sent up the cable which carries the AUDIO signal.

PHONO
A small audio co-axial cable plug.

PIC SYNC
The proprietary name of a tabletop film editing machine manufactured by 'ACMADE' in which the film and various sound tracks are laid side by side on a sprocket wheeled mechanism for matching or synchronising the pictures and the sound. The results being monitored on a small translucent screen and heard on a small monitor speaker

PICK-UP
1. The filming or recording of a camera shot at the end of a sequence for later editing into that sequence.
2. The restarting of a sequence of shots,'picking up' from where the shooting or recording stopped.

PIECE TO CAMERA
A commentary spoken whilst looking straight to camera.

PIERROT
A device which allows the 'GRABBING' of TV images
for the purpose of generating hand drawn silhouettes or
MATTES by use of an electronic pen and tablet.

PILOT
A trial TV programme of a SERIES.

PILOT TONE
An audio reference signal recorded by certain ATRs to
enable them to be synchronised to film cameras or
other equipment.

PIN REGISTERED
The precise locating of film FRAMES in the GATE of a
camera or TELECINE machine by means of the
PERFORATIONS engaging in accurately machined
pins.

PIXEL
The smallest element on a TV raster display. (Picture
element).

PLACE WITH CARE
A programme scheduling category.

PLAYLIST
A list of items or programmes to be played from an
automated audio or video player. Generally inputted via
a VDU terminal.

PLUG
1. A cable connector with pins.
2. The favourable promotion of a commercial item
during a discussion programme.

PLUGE (plooj)
Picture Line Up Generating Equipment. An electronic
test signal used for the correct setting of brightness and
contrast of a video MONITOR.

PLUMBICON
The proprietary name of a lead oxide TV camera
pick-up tube manufactured by PHILIPS INDUSTRIES
of Holland. (From Latin – Plumbum, lead + Icon, image)

PO
1. PULL OUT, a script abbreviation.
2. Post Office.

POA
Production Office Assistant.

PODS
A scaffold pole–type camera mounting head adapter.

POGLE
Pandora's Other Grading system and Little Editor. A computerised TELECINE colour GRADING system with VTR control capabilities from Pandora International.

POINT OF VIEW
A camera shot from a performer's viewpoint.

PO JACK
A three wire cable plug of circular cross–section that can be easily inserted or removed from a JACK socket. Originally used by Post Office telephone operators for the rapid connection of telephone circuits.

POLECAT
A spring loaded expandable metal pole that can be positioned between walls or ceiling and floor for the mounting of LUMINAIRES whilst on location.

POLYPHOTO
A display of multiple TV images on a video screen.

PORTAPROMPT
A proprietary name for a device that allows a rolling script to be projected onto an angled semi-silvered mirror placed in front of a TV camera such that the presenter looks into the lens whilst reading the script.

POS
POSITIVE.

POSTERISATION
A DVE effect in which an image is generated from a limited palette of colours and hence resembles a poster print.

POST ROLL
The time between a video out edit point and the cessation of recording. It provides for another choice of out edit later than the previous attempt.

POST SYNC
The process of adding dialogue to a film after it has been shot. *see* ADR, LOOPING.

POV
POINT OF VIEW, a script abbreviation.

PPB
Party Political Broadcast

PPM
Peak Programme Meter, an audio level measuring device of specific ballistics designed to indicate signal peaks rather than average levels.

PPS
Post Production Suite. A computerised videotape edit suite where programme material is edited together using various sophisticated VIDEO and AUDIO HARDWARE.

PPV
Pay Per View, television viewing by subscription.

PRACTICAL
A PROP that operates, eg a standard lamp that lights.

PRE-FADE
To play a tape or DISC from a prearranged cue point with the output faded down such that the item finishes when required, the fader being opened when required.

PRE- ROLL
The point from which a film machine or tape player must be run to achieve normal running speed prior to the required material.

PRES
Presentation. The department concerned with feeding the studio programmes, COMMERCIALS and on-air PROMOTIONS to the transmitters.

PRESTEL
The BT videotext system.

PREVIEW
1. The MONITOR in a studio GALLERY which displays
the next source to be output from the VISION MIXER.
2. The viewing of a film or programme to interested
parties prior to transmission or release.

PRINT
A positive film taken from a master negative or
INTERNEG.

PRINT THAT!
An indication by a DIRECTOR of a satisfactory TAKE.

PRINT THROUGH
The process of the magnetic signal on a layer of audio
or videotape leaking through onto the adjacent layers
on the reel.

PRIVATE WIRE
A dedicated BT telephone circuit.

PROC AMP
Processing Amplifier, a VIDEO amplifier which
removes the SYNCHRONISING PULSES from a video
signal and replaces them with locally generated sync
pulses.

PROCTOR
A large wheeled camera mount for use on rough
ground.

PROD CAP
A CAPTION which appears at the end of a programme
containing the trade mark or LOGO of the production
company.

PROD SEC
A secretary attached to a production to handle all the
clerical aspects.

PRODUCER
The person who exercises ultimate control over all
aspects of the production of a programme.

PROM(O)
Short excerpts of a forthcoming programme edited
together to form a teaser.

PROPS
A stage or studio property. Any article except costumes
and scenery used in a production.

PROTECTION COPY
A copy of an edited MASTER tape which is produced
immediately after the master has been completed. It is
used as a back up in the event of damage to, or loss of
the original.

PRS
The Performing Rights Society. An association of
authors, musicians and publishers engaged in the
collection of ROYALTIES for the public performance of
the works of its members.

PSC
Portable Single Camera. The shooting of programme
material in the manner of film but using a video camera
instead.

PTC
PIECE TO CAMERA.

PTP
A Pre-Transmission (call of nature.)

PULL
To discontinue a programme during its production or
transmission.

PULL BACK
To move a camera on its PED further from its subject in
view.

PULL FOCUS
To change optical focus from from one subject to
another in a camera image.

PULL OUT
1. PULL BACK
2. To widen the field of view of a camera by means of a ZOOM lens.

PUNCH UP
To select a picture source on a VISION MIXER.

PUP
A 1KW studio lamp

PUSH
To increase the contrast ratio of an underexposed film by overdevelopment in the processing laboratory.

P/V
PREVIEW, a script abbreviation.

PWC
PLACE WITH CARE, a script abbreviation.

PYTHON
The proprietary name of a counterbalanced 21 foot long camera boom arm which can be attached to various wheeled or fixed supports.

Q

Q-DOT
See CUE DOT.

QUADRUPLEX
The original ANALOGUE VT format developed by the
AMPEX corporation in 1956 which uses four video
heads to transversely scan 2" wide videotape.

QUAD SPLIT
A special VIDEO effect in which the TV scene is
divided into four rectangles each containing a complete
picture of reduced size.

QUANTEL
'QUAntised TELevision', a manufacturer of DIGITAL
TV HARDWARE.

QUARTER INCH
A generic term for an AUDIO tape recorder which uses
¼" wide audio tape on open reels.

R-Y
One of the two CHROMINANCE signals generated in
an ENCODED colour TV system, formed by subtracting
the brightness signal (Y) from the Red signal.
Producing a chrominance signal in this fashion ensures
that no brightness information is carried by the
chrominance signal and the chrominance signal is zero
when a monochrome image is transmitted.

RACK
To adjust the exposure of a TV camera.

RACK BAR
The black lines between the individual film frames on a
reel of film. Also known as frame bars.

RACK DOWN
To reduce the exposure of a TV camera.

RACKS
A term used to describe the department in a TV studio
facility concerned with the maintenance and exposure
of TV cameras and studio systems.

RACK UP
1. To increase the exposure of a TV camera.
2. To put a film in register with the gate aperture of a
TELECINE machine or projector such that the black
frame bars between frames are not visible on the
projected image.

RADIO CHECK
A TV receiver at an OUTSIDE BROADCAST location
which is used to check that the outside broadcast is
being transmitted on air.

RADIO LINKS
Super high frequency radio transmissions which are
used to convey VIDEO and AUDIO signals from a
remote location to a TV studio centre.

RADIO MIKE
A 'wireless' microphone.

RAI
Radiotelevisione Italiana. The Italian state broadcasting
organisation.

RAINBOW
A SOFTWARE enhancement to HARRY that provides
complete control over the colour and contrast of an
image.

RAM
RANDOM ACCESS MEMORY.

RAMCORDER
A DIGITAL VIDEO recorder which stores images in
RAM.

RANDOM ACCESS EDITING
A method of editing whereby VIDEO images are
converted into DIGITAL data which are then stored on
high capacity WINCHESTER DISK drives. The disks
allow random access to the stored images, unlike
videotape which has to SPOOL to the required image
before it can be accessed.

RANDOM ACCESS MEMORY
A microchip mass storage device designed in such a
manner that the information it contains can be
accessed without the need to instigate a search from
the beginning. It is constructed as a matrix of locations
each of which has a unique address which data can be
written to or read from.

RANGE EXTENDER
A supplementary lens inserted in the optical path of a
ZOOM lens to extend the working range of the lens,
now usually contained in the ZOOM lens package.

RASTER
The pattern of horizontal lines on a TV screen or picture monitor from which the scanned image is reconstructed.

RATIO (SHOOTING)
The relation of film or tape used, to film or tape appearing in the completed programme.

RATIONALISED PRINT
The reprinting of a feature film onto modern film STOCK in an ASPECT RATIO suitable for use in TV.

RAW STOCK
Unexposed film or unused videotape.

RDAT
Rotary Head DIGITAL Audio Tape, a helical scan recorder which records audio in DIGITAL form.

REAL TIME
Actual clock time.

REACTION SHOT
A camera shot used to illustrate a performer's reaction to an event or speech in a scene.

RE-VAMP
To re-use existing scenery for another production by superficial alterations, eg by repositioning or repainting.

READ ONLY MEMORY
A preprogrammed memory circuit whose contents cannot be altered by the user.

READ THROUGH
The first stage in a drama production when the artists and production team meet for the first time, generally in a rehearsal room.

RECCE
A preproduction examination of a location by the DIRECTOR, UNIT MANAGER and other interested personnel.

RED–HEAD
A 750–800W open faced lamp.

THE RED (PHONE)
A private telephone link serving the MCRs of all broadcasting organisations on a NETWORK. It is used by transmission staff to cope with unforeseen events and the exchange of late information.

RED STAR
A high priority parcel delivery service operated by British Rail which is regularly used by broadcasters and facilities companies for the movement of videotapes.

REGISTRATION
The accurate superimposition of the separate primary coloured images from a multitube TV camera to produce a full colour picture free from colour fringing.

REMOTE
A programme source from outside a facility's transmission centre, eg an OB or programme transmission from another broadcaster on a NETWORK.

RENDER
The production of solid computer generated images from outline guide images and other graphic instructions.

REPOS
Reposition, a script abbreviation.

RESIDUALS
Payments awarded to contracted writers, actors, musicians and directors who have contributed to a programme which is repeated or sold overseas.

REVEAL
A video transition in which an electronic CAPTION appears in stages over an existing picture, eg football results.

REVERB
Reverberation, an echo effect, natural or electronically generated.

REVERSE MUSIC CIRCUIT
A high quality BT circuit from the programme destination to the programme source for use in interviews etc.

REUTERS
An international news agency

REVERSAL
A camera shot taken from the opposite angle of the main shot.

RF
Radio Frequency.

RGB
The three primary colours Red, Green and Blue from which the colour spectrum is produced in a colour TV system.

RHUBARB
Indistinctive background chatter from EXTRAS in a production.

RIDE
To constantly adjust the operational controls of audio and video equipment during programme making whilst monitoring the results of the actions.

RIFLE MIKE
A specialised, highly directional microphone often used for ENG and filming work in order to reduce unwanted sound pick-up.

RIP AND READ
A term used to describe a news story received straight from an agency teleprinter and read by a presenter without being rewritten or rehearsed.

ROADSHOW
A series of thematic OBs from different locations.

ROCK AND ROLL
The process of moving a tape to and fro on a playback machine to locate a cue point or edit.

ROF
Right Of (image) Frame.

ROLL BACK AND MIX
A video effect where a scene is videotaped using a stationary camera and which now becomes a playback source after being 'rolled back' or rewound. The original scene with some alteration becomes the 'to' source. When a MIX transition is carried out only the alteration is evident by its gradual appearance or disappearance.

ROLLER
A form of CAPTION which moves vertically across the screen, usually at the end of a programme, carrying the names of those principally involved in its production.

ROLLING AND LOCKED
A verbal indication from a VT operator that the VT machine has reached normal operating speed from rest and that material now being recorded is able to be reproduced satisfactorily.

ROLL TK
The command from a PA to a TK operator to initiate a TELECINE to achieve normal running speed before a pre-arranged time.

ROM
READ ONLY MEMORY

ROTOSCOPE
A procedure which projects a film a FRAME at a time on to a surface for hand tracing and consequent generation of still frame CELS for use in ANIMATION. Similar techniques are used with video images being captured on a PAINTBOX or similar device. Animation produced by this method is more realistic.

ROUGH CUT
A preliminary edit of a film or videotaped programme prior to the FINE CUT.

ROUTER
A device used for the routing and distribution of AUDIO and VIDEO signals around a facility.

ROYALTIES
Payments to authors and composers from the proceeds resulting from the sale or performance of their work.

RS232C
An internationally agreed DIGITAL interconnecting standard used for the bidirectional transmission of data in serial form over short distances using a 25 pin plug and socket.

RS422
An internationally agreed DIGITAL interconnecting standard used for the bidirectional transmission of high speed data in serial form over distances of up to 4000 feet using a 9 pin plug and socket. It is more immune to interference than the RS232C standard.

RSD
Removable Storage Disk, a self contained HARD DISK storage system which can be easily removed from its associated equipment.

RT
A mobile or portable voice Receiver/Transmitter.

RTBF
Radio Television Belge de la Communauté Culturelle Francaise. The Belgian state broadcaster which broadcasts in French.

RTE
Radio Telefis Eireann, the Irish state broadcasting organisation.

RTL
Radio Television Luxembourgoise, a commercial radio and television broadcaster based in Luxembourg.

RTP
Radio Televisao Portuguesa, the Portuguese national television broadcaster.

RTS
The Royal Television Society.

RUBBER NUMBERS
EDGE NUMBERS, printed every foot (6" ON 16mm) on film and sound sections to aid in the locating and synchronising of the picture and sound material during editing.

RUNDOWN
An on-air MENU of the programmes to be transmitted.

RUNNER
A general assistant of a film or video UNIT.

RUNNING ORDER
A chronological list of the programme items occurring in a production.

RUNNING AND STABLE
A verbal indication from a VT operator that a VT machine has reached normal operating speed from rest and that material now being recorded is able to be reproduced satisfactorily.

RUN THROUGH
An attempt at a complete rehearsal.

RUN UP
The time taken for a piece of equipment to reach normal operating speed.

RUN VT
The command from a PA to a VT operator to initiate a VTR to achieve play speed before a prearranged time.

RUSHES
Sequences of film print received immediately after processing by the laboratory.

RX
1. Receiver.
2. Recorded.

RYLEY
An electronic CAPTION generator.

S4C
Sianel Pedwar Cymru (Welsh), Channel Four
Television for Wales.

SAFE ACTION AREA
An area of approximately 90% of a TV screen which is
normally seen on an OVERSCANNED domestic TV
receiver or MONITOR.

SAFE TITLE AREA
An area of approximately 80% of a TV screen within
which all GRAPHICS and text must be positioned in
order to be seen on an OVERSCANNED domestic TV
receiver or MONITOR.

SAFETY FREEZE
A FREEZE FRAME at the end of an edited INSERT in
a programme which allows for the reaction time of the
VISION and sound mixers when selecting the next
source.

SAFETY SHOT
Generally a wide angle shot of a scene or location
which is used by DIRECTORS and EDITORS in post
production when there is no other shot available.

SANS SERIF
A plain typographic FONT with no finishing strokes.

SAT
Satisfactory Any Time, a programme viewing category.

SATURATION
The purity of, or absence of white from a colour.

SATURATED GRID
A matrix of girders in a studio ceiling which supports
LUMINAIRES in sufficient numbers to avoid having to
reposition them for different productions.

SB
Simultaneous Broadcast, a programme, generally of
musical content, that is broadcast simultaneously on
FM STEREO radio and TV.

SBC
The Swiss Broadcasting Corporation.

SCANNER
1. An O.B. mobile production control room.
2. The rotating cylinder in a VTR or VCR which carries
the VIDEO HEADS.

SCANSAT
A DBS communications satellite broadcasting to
Scandinavia.

SCART
A 21 pin plug and socket used to connect an auxiliary
piece of equipment such as a video recorder to a TV
receiver to ensure optimum quality of reproduction.
Named after the French Society of Radio and
Television Manufacturers — Syndicat des Constucteurs
D'Appareils Radio Recepteurs et Televiseurs.

SCENE DOCK
An area set aside for the storage of SCENERY.

SCENE HAND
A member of a studio crew responsible for the
positioning and movement of SCENERY.

SCENIC ARTIST
An artist who paints distant views on a CYC or FLAT
which are seen through the doors or windows of a SET.

SCENERY
Painted FLATS and replicas of three dimensional
structures made from inexpensive materials such as
plaster, fibreglass or wood.

SCENESYNC
The proprietary name of a device that synchronises the movements of two camera PAN and TILT heads for use in a CHROMA KEY effect, one camera shooting the foreground subject in the CHROMA KEY set and the other camera shooting the background subject matter. The synchronised camera movements give the impression that the composite picture is only one subject by retaining perspective and depth.

SCH
SUBCARRIER to HORIZONTAL SYNC timing relationship, a critical timing measurement which must be maintained to produce disturbance-free video edits.

SCHWERM
A manufacturer of gyroscopically stabilised lens mountings for helicopter borne cameras.

SCOOP
A 500 watt, soft light studio LUMINAIRE.

SCOPE
1. CINEMASCOPE.
2. OSCILLOSCOPE.

SCOTTISH
The ITV programme contractor for the central region of Scotland.

SCRATCH TAPE
A short length of videotape.

SCRATCH TRACK
A poor quality sound track used for timing and cueing purposes in production or POST PRODUCTION. It is replaced by the proper mixed sound track in POST PRODUCTION when available.

SCREENING
A viewing of a film by interested parties.

SCRIM
Metal or fibreglass gauze placed in front of a lamp to provide diffuse light.

SCSI
Small Computer Systems Interface. A recognised standard method of connecting peripherals to a computer.

SDR
Special Discretion Required, a programme viewing category.

SECAM
SEquential Couleur Avec Memoire (French), sequential colour with memory, the 625 line colour TV system developed in France.

SECTION
Programme material that is not complete in itself, but which is edited together with other sections to form an INSERT to a programme or a complete programme.

SEGUE(SEGWAY)
A seamless transition from one movement or piece of music to another.

SELL
To offer an AUDIO or VIDEO circuit to a recipient for assessment.

SELVYT
A specialised cleaning and polishing cloth used in a film handling environment.

SENNHEISER
A German manufacturer of of film and TV audio equipment. Renowned for their highly directional microphones.

SEP MAG
Separate Magnetic, the playing of film sound on a separate reel of magnetic tape with SPROCKET HOLES which is run in synchronism with the pictures.

SERIF
The fine finishing strokes at the ends of the main strokes of a typographical character.

SET
An arrangement of studio scenery and PROPS.

SET UP
1. A camera and/or lighting arrangement.
2. The difference between BLANKING signal level and the black level signal of active video.

SFX
1. Sound effects,
2. Special effects, script abbreviations.

SHADING
An optical or electronic shortcoming in a imaging device which results in a variation of brightness across the image.

SHADING CORRECTOR
An electronic system in a camera or TELECINE which corrects SHADING errors.

SHARP
Optically (and electronically) in focus.

SHASH
Absolute noise, total absence of VIDEO and/or AUDIO signals resulting in 'a snowstorm' on the screen and hissing on sound.

SHEDDING
The loss of magnetic oxide from audio or video tape.

SHOTGUN MIKE
A specialised, highly directional microphone often used for ENG and filming work in order to reduce unwanted sound pick-up.

SHOOTING RATIO
The ratio of film exposed in the camera to film appearing in the final programme.

SHORT END
The videotape remaining on a reel after the removal of a substantive portion.

SHOT BOX
A device on a TV camera that allows the selection of
preset lens angles from a ZOOM lens at the push of a
button.

SHOTLISTER
A PC based logging system that produces a graphic
model of an editing decision list from OFF-LINE
videotapes, showing the video and audio tracks
vertically side by side on the screen.
The vertically scrolling video and audio tracks contain
the edit in and out TIMECODES with text comments
and can be easily fine tuned before being converted to
an industry standard edit list for downloading into an
ON- LINE edit controller.

SHOW PRINT
The final or transmission print of a negative film.

SHOWREEL
1. A videotape compilation of programme SECTIONS
to illustrate a company's programme catalogue to
potential buyers.
2. A videotape compilation of programme SECTIONS
edited by an individual editor. Used as an indicator of
their skill to potential employers.

SHUTTLE
The process of moving film or tape at high speed.

SI
Station Ident, a company's ' on-air ' LOGO or
trademark.

SIMON CRANE/HOIST
A lorry mounted hydraulic platform which can be raised
up to 30 metres above ground for the positioning of
cameras for high angle shots. Also used for the
positioning of microwave transmitters or receivers
which require line of sight for correct operation.

SIMULCAST
A musical programme broadcast simultaneously on
STEREO FM radio and TV.

SINGLE
A vinyl disc for use on a record player which contains only one musical piece per side.

SINGLETON
A camera shot of an individual item or person.

SIS
1. Sound In Syncs, a system devised by the BBC for incorporating a sound signal in DIGITAL form within the unseen LINE SYNC pulse, thereby dispensing with the need for a separate audio circuit for programme distribution.
2. Satellite Information Services, a company which specialises in satellite communications.

SITCOM
A comedy SERIES with a regular cast of characters.

SIT DOWN
The reduction of the BLACK LEVEL of a VIDEO signal towards BLANKING LEVEL.

SKEW
The bending of vertical elements of a TV image due to incorrect RASTER scanning geometry or incorrect videotape tape tension.

SKIDS
A wheeled triangular base fixed to the legs of a tripod to allow movement.

SKYCAM
A lightweight remote camera suspended overhead its subject by means of crosswires whose lengths are simultaneously adjusted by computer controlled winches to enable rapid repositioning of the camera anywhere over the subject.

SKYLIFT
A lorry mounted hydraulic lifting platform capable of reaching up to 66 metres above ground.

SKYSHOT
A lorry mounted hydraulic lifting platform capable of reaching up to 27 metres above ground.

SLASH PRINT
An ungraded film print taken directly from an existing workprint rather than the master negative where image quality is not important. It is used for sound dubbing purposes etc. whilst the workprint is in the hands of the NEG CUTTER.

SLATE
An information board held in front of a camera to identify the material (shot number, TAKE etc.) about to be shot.
see CLAPPER BOARD

SLAVE
A VT machine recording a specific camera source rather than the mixed output of a VISION MIXER.

SLIDEFILE
The proprietary name of a device that stores still VIDEO images in the form of DIGITAL data for later recall.

SLIDE SCANNER
A device for producing a VIDEO signal from a 35mm photographic transparency.

SLOMO
SLOw MOtion, the replaying of a videotape at slower than normal play speed for effect or analysis.

SLUG
Black spacing inserted in between film or videotaped programme parts to allow for the insertion of other material eg COMMERCIALS without having to stop and restart the film or videotape.

SMEAR
The blending of the detail transitions in an image due to poor low frequency response of the video signal system.

SMPTE
The Society of Motion Picture and Television Engineers
(USA.)

SMPTE LEADER
A standardised film countdown leader designed by the
SMPTE containing visual and audible cueing
information.

SNG
Satellite News Gathering. The acquisition of news
material from remote locations by using a geostationary
telecommunications satellite to relay the material to the
newsroom.

SNOOT
A tapering cylindrical shield fitted to a lamp to reduce
the width of lightbeam.

SNOW
What VIDEO noise looks like.

SNV
Satellite News Vehicle, a vehicle which contains the
necessary equipment to transmit news material to a
geostationary communications satellite for onward
routing.

SOAP
A melodramatic serial programme with a regular cast
of players involved in everyday situations, the first of
which was 'The Goldbergs' sponsored by Procter and
Gamble, an American soap manufacturer.

SOF
Sound On/Off Film, a script abbreviation.

SOFT
Optically or electronically not in sharp focus.

SOFTWARE
A sequence of instructions given to a computer
processor in order to allow it to carry out a task.

SOFT WIPE
A WIPE effect where the transition between the images
is not a well defined hard edge but a gradual transition.

SOLARISATION
1. LUMINANCE — a VIDEO effect where the
LUMINANCE signal is distorted to produce images of
bright highlights and deep shadows.
2.CHROMINANCE — a VIDEO effect where the
CHROMINANCE signal is distorted to produce images
with an absence of pastel shades.

SOLID STATE
An electronic device or system which is based on
semiconductor technology and does not contain any
thermionic vacuum devices.

SOLO
see A 34.

SONDOR
The proprietary name of a TELECINE machine film
sound reproducer.

SONG SHEET
A CAMERA SCRIPT.

SONY
A Japanese manufacturer of various broadcast and
domestic electronic equipment, colloquially refers to a
LOW BAND U-MATIC type VIDEOCASSETTE
recorder.

SOT
1. Start Of Tape, a script abbreviation.
2. Sound Off Tape, a script abbreviation.

SOUND DUB
1. The mixing together of the various sound tracks
associated with a piece of film to produce the complete
film sound track.
2. Making a copy of one audio tape from another.

SOUND POST PRODUCTION
The producing of the final programme sound by the remixing of audio sources with the addition of music, sound effects, and VOs as required, and the rectification of sound flaws either side of a picture edit.

SOUNDSTATION
A DIGITAL audio production centre from Digital Audio Research.

SOVT
Sound Off/On VideoTape, a script abbreviation.

SPACER-LEADER
Blank film in a reel or video black on a videotape which is used to maintain programme timing and which will be replaced by material of the same length in the final edited version.

SPARKLE
1. Specks of dirt on a NEGATIVE film which appear as white dots on the print.
2. The twinkling effect on televised film pictures when excessive APERTURE CORRECTION has been introduced to improve the sharpness of the image.

SPARKLIES
Distinctive white dot-type interference on a TV picture from a satellite, due to insufficient signal arriving at the receiver.

SPARKS
An electrician.

SPECULAR
A dazzling light reflection from a highly reflective surface.

SPEED
An indication that a film camera or sound recorder has reached normal operating speed.

SPG
Synchronising Pulse Generator. An electronic timing device which produces accurately timed and shaped electronic pulses which are fed to all the image generating and processing equipment in a facility to ensure that the scanning process remains synchronised from the camera to the domestic TV receiver.

SPILL
1. Unwanted overlapping light sources.
2. Unwanted sounds picked up by a microphone designated to another source.

SPIN OFF
Merchandising and other productions resulting from a film or programme success.

SPIN TIMING
A method of timing the duration of a videotaped programme by spooling from start to finish and noting the times on the VTR tape timer.

SPLIT EDIT
A videotape edit in which the VIDEO and AUDIO edits occur at different times.

SPLITTER
A one input, two output cable adapter.

SPLIT TRACKS
A procedure in VIDEO editing where one of the DCM tracks has been used to record material which is different from the other and consequently the single track containing the final programme audio must be correctly identified before use.

SPREAD
An instruction from a DIRECTOR to a presenter or performer to lengthen an item for programme timing purposes.

SPROCKET HOLES
The rectangular perforations along the edge of a film which are used in conjunction with toothed wheels for its transport though a camera or projector and registration in the GATE.

SPOT
A position in a RUNNING ORDER.

SPOT CHECK
Verification of a recording by sample checking selected parts of the tape.

SPOT EFFECTS
Sound effects which are played from a SPOT PLAYER.

SPOT PLAYER
An endless audio tape loop CARTRIDGE used for sound effects, COMMERCIALS or JINGLES which can be rapidly cued.

SPOT REEL
A lightweight reel containing up to 10 minutes of videotape which is generally used for the trafficking of COMMERCIALS or other short programme material between companies.

SQUAWK BOX
An intercom system between a studio GALLERY and support area (eg a newsroom).

SQUEAK
To adjust the frequency response of an amplifier or circuit.

SQUEEZEZOOM
The proprietary name for an early DVE manufactured by VITAL industries.

SSVR
Solid State Video Recorder. A device for the temporary recording of short sections of video material in DIGITAL memory during a video edit.

STABLE
An indication from a VT operator that a VT machine
has reached normal operating speed.

STACK
The process in the data management system of a DLS
that enables a group of VIDEO STILL FRAMES to be
stored together in a sequence, that sequence being
recalled by its stack number.

STAGGER
The very first attempt at rehearsal for all concerned.
Tends to be stopped and started frequently for various
logistical reasons.

STAIRSTEPPING
The resultant reproduction of a sloping line as a
'STAIRSTEP' when generated on a DIGITAL display
system with ALIASING occurring. Most high quality
character generators possess anti-aliasing
SOFTWARE to overcome this problem.

STANDARDS CONVERTER
A specialised DIGITAL FRAME STORE which is used
to convert one TV system to another.

STARLIGHT
An enhancement to QUANTEL'S MIRAGE DVE which
generates a synthetic light source by using light and
shade modifiers on the image.

STARSHOT
The proprietary name of a lorry mounted hydraulic
lifting platform capable of reaching up to 52 metres
above ground level.

STEADICAM
The proprietary name of a camera operators harness
capable of damping out hand held camera movement
by means of springs and counterbalancing weights.

STEADIGATE
The proprietary name of a specialised TELECINE film GATE which accurately locates the film FRAME in its aperture by means of the PERFORATIONS engaging on accurately machined fixed pins. The film can only be used in ' STOP FRAME ' mode and not run at normal speed. Transferring film to videotape by this means ensures 'rock steady' film images without WEAVE or BOUNCE and allows recorded film to be intermarried with video images without any apparent relative image movement .

STEADIWAVE
A miniature portable microwave transmitter for use with a STEADICAM which eliminates the use of cables between camera and OB SCANNER.

STEENBECK
The proprietary name of a flatbed film editing and viewing machine.

STEREO
Stereophonic, the use of twin sound channels to produce an illusion of spatially distributed sound sources from two carefully positioned loudspeakers.

STICK
The retention of an image on a TV camera pick-up tube due to prolonged exposure to a bright subject.

STICTION
A term coined to describe the adhesion of videotape to the HEAD DRUM of a VTR caused by static electricity or poor tape lubrication.

STILL STORE
A device that stores still TV images by converting them into DIGITAL data and storing the data on WINCHESTER DISKS under a management system.

STILLS
Photographs.

STING
1. A short, vibrant musical piece used for impact.
2. A short electronic or optically generated animated
visual.

STOCK
A generic term for film or videotape.

STOCKSHOT
Images of a general nature, produced for the use of
others and held in a library.

STORYBOARD
A sequence of sketches or other artwork outlining the
visual aspects of a production.

STRAPCAP
A text CAPTION superimposed on a narrow horizontal
coloured band.

STRAPLINE
See STRAPCAP.

STRETCH
To prolong or lengthen an item.

STRIATIONS
A fault condition which causes vertical intensity banding
on the left hand side of a TV picture.

STRIKE
To remove a PROP or item of scenery from a SET.

STRINGER
A freelance news gatherer, eg a cameraperson or
journalist.

STRIPE
1. A narrow band of magnetic material applied along
the vertical edge of a film for the purpose of recording
and replaying of sound.
2. The process of recording COLOUR BLACK,
CONTROL TRACK and TIMECODE on a videotape as
a prerequisite to INSERT editing.

STROBING

The visual distortion of moving subjects being filmed or televised, due to interference between the picture rate and the rate of movement of the subject, generating an unwanted visual product, e.g. spoked wagon wheels apparently revolving in the opposite direction to the motion of the wagon. *See* ALIASING. Not to be confused with CROSS COLOUR.

STUDER

A Swiss manufacturer of audio tape recorders widely used by broadcasters and facilities companies.

STV

SCOTTISH TeleVision.

SUBCARRIER

The signal that conveys the colour information in a COMPOSITE ENCODED colour VIDEO signal.

SUBLIMINAL

A now illegal technique used in advertising where one frame of unrelated material is inserted into a straightforward sequence. This is not perceived by the conscious but may influence the subconscious. It is strictly forbidden by the regulations governing the broadcasting of commercials and is very suspect elsewhere.

SUN GUN

A battery powered hand held lamp used mostly on documentaries and news filming.

SUPER

Superimposition. The superimposition of one picture upon another such that both pictures remain visible, eg CAPTIONS over a background picture. Also refers to a CAPTION which is KEYED into a background picture.

SUPER TROUPER

A very large follow spotlight.

SVHS

Super VHS, an improved version of the VHS format.

SWC
Schedule With Care, a programme viewing category.

SWEETENING
An audio post production process where audio problems are rectified with the possible addition of simple effects.

SWISH PAN
A rapid horizontal camera movement such that the image becomes blurred.

SWITCHER
An American term for a VISION MIXER control panel.

SWOOP
A dynamic move of a TV image in three dimensions by utilising perspective in a DIGITAL VIDEO EFFECTS system.

SYNCHRONISER
A VIDEO image FRAME STORE which stores images which can then be outputted in synchronism with other image sources.

SYNCS
Synchronising pulses, the portion of an ENCODED COMPOSITE VIDEO signal which occurs during BLANKING and is used to synchronise the scanning operation of the cameras, monitors and other equipment in a facility. The synchronising pulses are transmitted along with the VIDEO information to allow the video image to be correctly reconstructed.

SYNC MARK
A visual indication, generally a large X, on film and sound-track LEADERS which indicates accurate synchronisation.

TABS
A theatrical stage curtain which opens horizontally from the centre.

TAF
TELECINE Analysis Film, a test film for performance verification of a telecine machine.

TAG
The last line of a dialogue which is used for cueing and timing purposes.

TAIL
The end of a reel of film or tape.

TAIL OUT
A film wound on a reel such that the end of the film leaves the reel first, ie after it has been run on a film machine.

TAIL SLATE
See END SLATE.

TAKE
Any of a series of attempts at filming or recording the same scene.

TALKBACK
An inter - area communication system.

TBA
1. To Be Announced, a script abbreviation.
2. To Be Arranged, a script abbreviation.

TBC
TimeBase Corrector, a device for smoothing out the
mechanical timing instabilities of a VTR to produce
stable TV pictures.

TC
1. TIMECODE
2. Television Centre (BBC) Wood Lane, London.
3. Transmission Controller.(or Presentation Director)
The person in the presentation department of a TV
broadcasting organisation responsible for the
co - ordination of all programming material sent to the
transmitters.

TCG
TIMECODE Generator.

TCR
TIMECODE Reader.

TEASE(R)
A short preview of programme material to follow.

TECHNICOLOR
An early colour motion picture system which recorded
images as three simultaneous monochrome negatives
each receiving the red, green and blue filtered light
from the subject. Monochrome prints of the three
negatives were simultaneously projected through red
green and blue filters and registered on the screen to
produce the full colour image.

TECH RUN
An early rehearsal of a production in the studio with all
involved, to identify and rectify any technical problems.

TELECINE
A machine in the form of a film transport with
associated electronics which produces VIDEO images
from film.

TELEPORT
A centre for the uplinking of TV signals to geostationary
communications satellites.

TELEPROMPT
The proprietary name of a device that projects a rolling script onto an angled semi-silvered mirror system positioned in front of the camera lens, so that the presenter looks at the lens whilst reading the script.

TELEREC
Telerecording, the process of filming television programmes for archival or interchange purposes.

TELETEXT
The transmission of text and graphics to TV receivers by inserting data in the TV signal which appears at the top of picture frame, but outside the picture area. It is then decoded for displaying on the TV screen.

TELETHON
A portmanteau word, TELEvision maraTHON. A long TV programme in which performers supply their talent free of charge and presenters persuade the public to indulge in fund raising activities for charitable causes.

THREE PERF
A 35mm film system which uses a film frame three PERFORATIONS high instead of four with the consequential saving of 25% in film stock.

THROW
1.'Throw to....A.N.Other.'
An instruction from a programme DIRECTOR to a presenter or commentator to complete his dialogue and generate a verbal link to the following presenter or event.
2. The useful working distance from a light source to the subject.

THUNDER SHEET
A large sheet of thin metal or formica which generates the sound of thunder when flexed rapidly.

TIFFEN
A manufacturer of optical filters for cameras.

TIGHTEN
To ZOOM in on a subject for dramatic or visual emphasis.

TILT
The pivoting of a camera in a vertical direction.

TIMECODE
An electronic timing signal recorded along the length of a tape as an aid in locating programme material on the tape.

TITLE KEY
A VIDEO KEY effect where parts of a background or primary picture are replaced by a CAPTION. The CAPTION can be modified by using the various options on the KEYER to colour or edge the CAPTION.

TK
BEEB term for TELECINE.

TNC
Threaded Nut Connector, a type of video cable connector.

TOBLERONE
A scenic device consisting of multiple triangular prisms which rotate together to present three different backgrounds to the camera. (Named after the triangular shaped Swiss chocolate bar.)

TODTC
Time Of Day TIMECODE.

TOF
Top Of (image) Frame.

TOIL
Time Off In Lieu (of overtime payments).

TOM
Technical Operations Manager.

TONE
A fixed frequency audio reference signal of known level, used to adjust audio equipment and check audio signal paths.

TOPICALS
Current, newsworthy material used in light entertainment programmes.

TOPSY
Telecine Operational Programming SYstem. An obsolete TELECINE film programming system. The term is still used by some to mean the automatic colour correcting, panning and ZOOMING of films on a TELECINE machine using a computerised film programmer.

TRACK
1. The physical movement of a camera on its PED or DOLLY towards or away from the subject being televised.
2. The specified area on a film or videotape which carries information.

TRACK LAYING
The process of matching the various film sound tracks for synchronism with the picture.

TRAILS
1. On-air promotions of forthcoming programmes.
2. A DVE effect in which a manipulated TV image leaves a trail from its starting position on the screen.

TRAMLINES
Parallel scratch lines along the length of a film caused by protrusions or foreign material in the film path of the various film handling equipment.

TRANNY
A single positive photographic film image generally mounted in a holder for viewing or projection.

TRANSFER
The process of recording filmed programme material onto videotape for editing or transmission purposes.

TVR

TRANSPONDER
A portmanteau word, TRANSmitter, resPONDER. A radio frequency transmitter which is activated by the reception of a predetermined signal. Used in geostationary communications satellites and unmanned terrestrial transmitters.

TRAVELLING MATTE
A film printing process where a silhouette mask of a foreground subject is produced to blank out that area on another picture, thus allowing introduction of a foreground subject of one picture into another picture.

TRAWL
A special announcement made to attract viewer response, usually in connection with a future programme (eg contestants for a forthcoming quiz programme.)

TRIMS
The short lengths of film and sound removed after a section of film has been edited.

TROMBONING
The continuous and unwarranted use of a ZOOM lens.

TS
Technical Supervisor, the person responsible for the technical aspects of a studio production.

TTT
TYNE TEES Television.

TURKEY
A film or programme that is a critical or financial flop.

TURNOVER (The cranking handle!!)
The command to set a film camera or sound recorder running.

TVR
TeleVision Rating. A figure which indicates the percentage of households in a selected area who are viewing a programme, averaged over the programme duration.

TV STANDARDS
Three major TV systems exist worldwide, NTSC, PAL and SECAM. They are not compatible and video material in one system has to undergo standards conversion via a sophisticated DIGITAL FRAME STORE before it can be used in another.

TWEAK
A small adjustment of a control.

TWEAKER
1. A small screwdriver.
2. A compulsive adjuster of controls.

TWEETER
A small loudspeaker used to reproduce high frequencies in the audio spectrum. Generally used in conjunction with a WOOFER.

TWO POP
A shot burst of audio tone on a film leader which indicates two seconds before the start of film sound.

TWO SHOT
A camera shot of two individuals or items.

TX
Transmission.

TX PRINT
The final graded colour print from an edited colour negative film.

TYNE TEES
The ITV broadcaster serving the north east region of England.

U
1. UPSTAGE, a script abbreviation.
2. The signal generated by modulating SUBCARRIER
with the 'scaled down' or weighted (B—Y) colour
difference signal in the PAL ENCODED COMPOSITE
colour television signal.
3. A standardised height unit of 19" wide equipment
racking. A 'U' equals 1.75".

UFB
Unfit For Broadcast.

UHF
Ultra High Frequency. Electromagnetic radio waves in
the frequency range of 300 to 3000 MHz. Used for the
broadcasting of television signals in the UK as well as
other traffic.

ULCER
A piece of opaque material with irregular holes which is
placed in front of a LUMINAIRE to produce patterned
illumination.

ULSTER
The ITV broadcaster in Northern Ireland.

ULTIMATTE
A special VIDEO effects device that allows a
foreground subject on one picture to be added to
another picture by matting (electronically cancelling)
out the unwanted background of the picture that
contains the foreground subject.

U-MATIC
A 3/4" VIDEOCASSETTE recording system.
There are two standards, LOW BAND, for viewing and archival purposes, and HIGH BAND which produces enhanced pictures for ENG purposes.

UNDERCRANK
A term used to describe the slow running of film in a motion picture camera which results in the speeding up of the action when the film is projected at normal speed.

UNDERRUN
A programme or scene which finishes earlier than its specified time.

UNDERSCAN
The viewing on a VIDEO MONITOR of all the transmitted video signal including BLANKING and SYNCS which are not seen on a domestic television receiver.

UNDERSTUDY
An artist who has fully rehearsed and is available to replace another artist in a production when the need arises.

UNILATERAL
Exclusive use of a satellite TRANSPONDER by a broadcaster or communications facility.

UNIT
A film or video production crew.

UNITAB
Universal Transfer roll A roll B system.
A method of transferring film to videotape by electronically cutting between two TELECINE machines containing A and B rolls which are synchronised by TIMECODE.

UNIT MANAGER
A member of a film or video production team who is in overall charge of the logistics and their costs.

UP GRAMS
The command from a director to a sound mixer to
FADE UP a music source.

UPLINK
An earth station to satellite transmission.

UPSTAGE
1. A performing area furthest from the camera or
theatre audience.
2. To dominate a scene by going OTT to the detriment
of the other players.

UP THE LINE
A programme or programme material played out from
another contractor on a TV NETWORK for later use.

UP TIME
A precise prearranged time between a
PRESENTATION DIRECTOR and a programme
source specifying when the programme should begin.

URSA
A FLYING SPOT type of TELECINE from Rank Cintel
with DIGITALLY controlled scanning RASTER and
VIDEO channels.

U/S
Unserviceable, useless.

USER BITS
Unassigned data BITS in the TIMECODE signal that
can be used for other information such as time, date,
TAKE number etc.

UTL
UP THE LINE.

V
1. Volt, the electrical unit of electromotive force.
2. The signal generated by modulating SUBCARRIER with the 'scaled down' or weighted (R-Y) colour difference signal in the PAL ENCODED television system.

VAC
Vertical Aperture Correction, the enhancement of edges on vertical picture information by electronic means, in order to subjectively improve picture detail.

VAR
Vision Apparatus Room, a centralised equipment room for a studio or facility.

VAULT
A specialised room with a controlled environment for the safekeeping of film and videotape.

VBV
Video Black Video. A method of previewing a VIDEO INSERT edit. The video of the original material is followed by a black segment representing the new video which is then followed by the original video again. Useful in determining FRAME accurate in and out edit points.

VCR
1. Vision Control Room. A studio control room where the images from cameras are adjusted for correct exposure by the vision control engineer in liaison with the LIGHTING DIRECTOR and programme DIRECTOR.
2. VIDEOCASSETTE RECORDER.

VDA
Video Distribution Amplifier. A VIDEO amplifier that accepts one input and delivers multiple identical outputs for distribution to various destinations.

VDU
Visual Display Unit. The TV monitor screen associated with a computer information system.

VECTOR MOVES
An enhancement to the ASTON CAPTION and ASTON 4 which produces horizontal WIPE effects and vertical picture moves to CAPTIONS.

VECTORSCOPE
A video waveform monitor that is configured to display the CHROMINANCE values of a TV signal on a polar scale.

VERTICAL BLANKING
The period between successive VIDEO FIELDS during which the electron scanning beam in a CRT is 'blanked out' to allow for the invisible retrace from the bottom of one FIELD to the top of the next.

VERTICAL INTERVAL
The period of 25 TV LINES in every FIELD during which no active picture information appears. It is analogous to film FRAME bars and is now widely used for the insertion of electronic test signals.

VERTICAL SYNC
A series of electronic pulses residing within the VERTICAL INTERVAL which are used to synchronise the beginning of each new FIELD.

VHF
Very High Frequency, the electromagnetic frequency spectrum from 30 to 300MHz. which is occupied by some radio transmissions

VHS
Video Home System, a domestic VIDEOCASSETTE
recorder system manufactured and licensed by the
Victor Company of Japan (JVC)

VIDEO
The electrical signal that produces an image on an
electronic display device.

VIDEO BOX
'Portacabins' containing a VIDEO camera and VIDEO
recorder where members of the general public can
personally record their comments on various subjects
for CHANNEL FOUR television.

VIDEOCASSETTE
A plastic protective enclosure for videotape which is
held on a supply reel. The tape is received back onto a
take up reel after passing over the various parts of a
videocassette recorder.

VIDEODISC
A playback-only disc onto which television images and
sound have been recorded for playback through a
domestic TV receiver or monitor. It has the advantage
over prerecorded videotape of rapid random access
and is widely used as an interactive teaching tool.

VIDEO KEY
A video effect where parts of one picture are replaced
by another *see* LUMINANCE KEY and CHROMA KEY.

VIDEO HEAD
An electromagnetic transducer which converts VIDEO
signals into a magnetic flux for retention on
magnetisable tape. The magnetised tape produces a
video signal when drawn past the head.

VIDEO SCOPE
A device which functions both as a VIDEO
WAVEFORM MONITOR and VECTORSCOPE by
displaying DIGITALLY generated video waveforms
over the related video image on any standard video
monitor.

VIDEO WALL
An array of picture monitors or TV screens with associated VIDEO switching to enable each monitor to display multiple identical images or a component tile of one large image.

VIDICON
A VIDeo camera pick up tube employing photoCONnductive material for the image target.

VIGNETTING
1. Corner shading or loss of corner optical resolution of a camera image by the intrusion of the LENS HOOD or other obstruction into the optical path.
2. The introduction of a mask into an optical system for the production of special effects (eg binocular effect).

VINTEN
1. A manufacturer of camera mounting heads and DOLLIES.
2. The proprietary name of a three wheeled, steer and CRAB studio camera pedestal mount.

VISC
Vertical Interval SubCarrier. A SUBCARRIER synchronising signal which occurs in the VERTICAL INTERVAL.

VISION MIXER
The person who selects picture sources under the instruction of the programme DIRECTOR using a device of the same name.

VISNEWS
An international news agency.

VISTA VISION
A wide screen film format obtained by using 35mm film horizontally rather than vertically. The image occupies the area of two standard film frames.

VITC
Vertical Interval Time Code. A VIDEO signal recorded outside picture area at the top of FRAME which contains a numerical address related to tape time or real time. It is used as an aid in locating image frames on the tape and it is the signal that computerised videotape edit controllers seek in order to acquire specific video image frames. It has the advantage over LTC of always being received as long as a picture is present, as LTC, being an AUDIO signal, requires tape motion.

VITS
Vertical Interval Test Signal. An electronic test signal inserted in the VERTICAL INTERVAL in order to check the integrity of a transmission path.

VJ
Video Jockey. A presenter who introduces video recordings of popular musical performers on satellite and cable TV.

VLAD
VINTEN Low Angle DOLLY.

VLSI
Very Large Scale Integration. A microchip which contains upwards of 16000 electronic components on a single chip of silicon crystal.

VLS
Very Long Shot, a script abbreviation.

VO
Voice Over, commentary added to pictures.

VOX POPS
Short informal interviews carried out with members of the public in the street. From the Latin, Vox Populi,'Voice of the people'.

VPR
Video Production Recorder, a generic name given to all 1" C FORMAT VTR machines manufactured by the AMPEX corporation.

VT(R)
VideoTape Recorder.

VT Clock
A countdown clock with programme identification
details which precedes all prerecorded material.

VU
Volume Units meter, an instrument used to measure
average AUDIO levels.

VVV
Video, Video, Video, a mode of previewing a VIDEO
INSERT edit. It consists of the originally recorded
material followed by the newly inserted material which
itself is followed by the original material.

W

W/A
WIDE ANGLE, a script abbreviation.

W/S
WIDE SHOT, a script abbreviation.

WALK ON
A WALK ON 1 is an EXTRA who is individually directed
but has no dialogue.
A WALK ON 2 is an EXTRA who is individually directed
and also has a few words of unimportant dialogue.

WALK THROUGH
A sequential but discontinuous rehearsal of a
production to allow for the identification and rectification
of problems.

WALKIE TALKIE
A hand held radio receiver/transmitter used regularly on
film and VIDEO shoots.

WALL BRACE
A telescopic wooden strut with metal hooks at each end
which engage in eyelets in scenic FLATS and metal
stage weights on the floor.

WALLET
A general purpose DIGITAL STILL STORE by Aston
Electronics capable of storing up to 33 full FRAME
images on its fixed HARD DISK and 35 on a RSD.

WARDROBE
The costume department of a production company.

WARM UP
The enlivening or briefing of a studio audience before transmission or recording by a stand-up comedian or other specially engaged person.

WARP
An optional facility on an ABEKAS A53D DVE that produces curved distortions to VIDEO images.

WATERSHED
A specified time, (generally 2100hrs) after which programmes suitable for adult viewing only may be broadcast.

WET HIRE
The hiring of equipment with operating personnel or GUARANTEE ENGINEER.

WAVEFORM MONITOR
A specialised OSCILLOSCOPE for the inspection and measurement of TV VIDEO signal waveforms.

WEAVE
Rhythmic sideways movement of a filmed image due to mechanical wear in the film or film transport.

WEMBLEY
The proprietary name of a camera mounting DOLLY used on OBs.

WET GATE
A device placed in the film path of a TELECINE machine or optical printer, which minimises the effect of scratches on a film image by flushing rapid drying fluid of the same refractive index as the film base across the film surface during exposure to the analysing light source.

WHITE BALANCE
The automatic or manual adjusting of the amplitude of
the Red, Green and Blue VIDEO signals of a TV
camera to produce a white image on a correctly
adjusted TV monitor whilst viewing a white test chart.
When carried out in conjunction with a black balance,
which is accomplished by adjusting the BLACK LEVEL
controls of the colour signals whilst the camera is
CAPPED-UP, a faithful colour image will be produced.

WHITE CLIP
An electronic threshold control which limits the
amplitude of a VIDEO signal in a system.

WHIP PAN
The rapid horizontal pivoting motion of a camera such
that the subject becomes blurred.

WIDE ANGLE
A camera shot in which the field of view is substantially
greater than that seen by a person.

WIDE SHOT
A panoramic view.

WIDE SCREEN
Reduced height pictures on a standard 35mm film
FRAME to give a different ASPECT RATIO to the
projected image.(Generally greater than 1.4:1)

WILD TRACK
An AUDIO recording of background ambient sounds
that is not synchronised to the camera at time of
filming.

WIMP
Windows, Icons, Mouse and Pull down menus.
A user friendly graphical interface between the user
and the operating system of a computer.

WINCHESTER
A high capacity HARD DISK data storage system comprising several disks or platters stacked in the same drive system and enclosed in an airtight container to exclude dust and dirt. The disks rotate continuously at high speed which causes a cushion of air to be formed between the recording heads and the disks. This causes the heads to fly very close to the surface of the disks without actually touching, which would lead to catastrophic failure. The proximity and number of heads, together with the speed of rotation of the disks all contribute to the packing density of the data and its speed of acquisition.

WIND GAG (or shield)
A microphone cover which minimises the effect of wind noise on the sound being received.

WINDOW DUB
A DUB of a videotape with its associated TIMECODE inlaid into the picture for logging purposes.

WINDOWING
The production of inter-layer gaps in a loosely wound film or videotape due to the film or tape continuing to spin on the reel when it is stopped suddenly. Also known as CINCHING.

WIND UP
A visual gesture from a FLOOR MANAGER in the form of circular movements with a pointed finger to a presenter or interviewer instructing them to conclude.

WING IT (Wing and a prayer)
Let's....To proceed without any rehearsal. Derived from the theatre, where performers who had failed to learn their lines would pin their script to the WINGS of the stage or any other convenient location.

WINGS
1. The unseen areas either side of a theatrical stage.
2. A scenery FLAT projecting onto the stage from the side.

WIPE
1. To erase a tape.
2. A film or VIDEO effect in which one image is gradually replaced by another at a boundary provided by a preselected pattern. As the wipe transition proceeds, the pattern edge moves until one image is completely replaced by the other.

WOOFER
A loudspeaker unit designed specifically to handle the low frequency end of the audio spectrum, generally used in conjunction with a TWEETER.

WORKPRINT
The print of a negative film section which is used by the film editor to produce a model of the complete production. It is used as a guide for the NEG CUTTER who produces the master negative from which all succeeding prints are made.

WORM
Write Once, Read Many times. An optical DISK storage system in which data are written to a silvered disk by blistering with a laser beam. The data, now permanently recorded, are recovered by reading the blisters in the silvering by a non-destructive laser beam. This type of storage finds its use in DIGITAL picture library archives.

WOW
Low frequency rhythmic variations in the speed of audio recording /playing equipment due to mechanical defects.

WRAP
"It's a".....Completion of a days shooting.

WRITE
The process of recording data onto a magnetic medium.

WRITE PROTECT
A mechanical guard which prevents data being recorded onto a magnetic medium.

WRITING SPEED
The speed at which information is transferred to a storage medium.

WTN
Worldwide Television News. A news agency partly owned by ITN.

WYSIWYG
What You See Is What You Get. An acronym for computer software applications which produce on a printer precisely what appears on the VDU screen.

X BAND
Microwave radio transmissions in the frequency range
5.2 to 10.9 GHZ which are used for the transmission of
VIDEO signals from remote locations to a studio
centre.

X-CALIBRE
A DVE by GML.

XCU
EXTREME CLOSE UP, a script abbreviation.

XF
CROSSFADE, a script abbreviation.

XFER
Transfer (film to videotape).

XLR
A locking, multipin, audio cable connector of circular
cross section.
X = common conductor, L = left conductor and R = right
conductor.

XLS
EXTREME LONG SHOT, a script abbreviation.

XT
EXtended Technology, an improved performance
version of the original IBM PC.

XY ZOOM
The electronic manipulation of the scanning RASTER
of a TELECINE machine which allows the magnification
and positioning of any part of a film image to be
displayed.

Y
The LUMINANCE or brightness component of a colour VIDEO signal, whether COMPOSITE or COMPONENT format. It is formed by adding together the Red, Green and Blue primary colour signals in the ratio of 30% Red, 59% Green and 11% Blue.

YAGI
A frequency selective directional aerial consisting of a horizontal tubular support on which are mounted numerous parallel rods or elements at specific distances depending on its use. Named after its Japanese inventor.

YASHMAK
A light diffuser covering the lower half of a LUMINAIRE. (From the veil worn by Arab women in public which covers the lower half of the face.)

Y Cr Cb
A complete set of SONY COMPONENT TV signals representing the LUMINANCE and CHROMINANCE values of a picture. *See* Cr and Cb

YELL
A TV news story without pictures.

YLE
Oy Yleisradio, the Finnish state broadcaster.

YORKSHIRE TV
The ITV franchise holder for the Yorkshire region of England.

YIQ
A set of LUMINANCE (Y) and CHROMINANCE (I&Q) signals in the American NTSC ENCODED colour TV system.

Y Pr Pb
A complete set of PANASONIC COMPONENT TV signals representing the LUMINANCE and CHROMINANCE values of a video image.

YTV
YORKSHIRE TeleVison.

YUV
A set of LUMINANCE (Y) and CHROMINANCE (U&V) signals in the PAL ENCODED colour TV system.

Z MODULATION
Intensity modulation of the trace on an
OSCILLOSCOPE.

ZAP
1. The act of changing channels rapidly on a domestic
TV receiver by use of a remote control handset.
2. The destruction of a delicate electronic component
due to a surge of static electricity.

ZDF
Zweites Deutsches Fernsehen, the second (West)
German national television network.

ZERO LEVEL
A reference audio level. It is used to verify the audio
equipment and the audio path of a facility. The scale of
a PPM indicates 4 when an audio signal dissipates 1
mW. in a 600 ohm load. ie 0 DBM.

ZEUS
A high quality TBC/picture processor manufactured by
the AMPEX corporation. It contains a FRAME STORE
which allows enhanced pictures at normal play speed
and smooth slow motion along with high quality freeze
FRAMES on all of the AMPEX VPR series of 1" C
FORMAT VTR machines.

ZIP
A character by character reveal of a CAPTION,
typewriter fashion.

ZIP PAN
The rapid movement of a camera in the horizontal
plane such that the image becomes blurred. Also
known as a swish pan.

ZITS
Short term image defects in a DIGITAL television system i.e. black spots on an image due to missing data BITS.

ZONES
The area of a TV screen is divided into zones both for maximum safe viewing area and qualitative assessment. Zone 1 is the area equal to 0.8 picture height, zone 2 is the area equal to picture width and zone 3 is the area outside zone 2.

ZOOM
1. A camera lens of continuously variable focal length.
2. The apparent movement towards or away from a subject by the use of a zoom lens or manipulation of the image by a DVE.